DISTRIBUTED CLOUD YUNFS

DISTRIBUTED CLOUD YUNFS
Concepts and Design

HONGLIANG ZHU

*To my wife, thank a lot for
your great contribution.*

CONTRIBUTORS

XIAOYUN,KONG   My wife, who draws all pictures of this book.

CONTENTS

LIST OF FIGURES

Listings

PREFACE

When talking about the design and implementation of a system most technical books are almost hard and boring. A reader need concentrates his energies on reading those hard technical books without any distraction. Though the reader may get knowledge from the books finally, he need to spend more time and more energy.

When I decide to write this book to introduce the YunFS, how to avoid boring and keep reading simple becomes my most important target. When we were still children, we usually learned the words by using cartoon pictures and stories, with those interesting cartoon pictures and stories, we knew the language step by step.

Figure 0.1   Bang on reading hard technical book.

This book is fulfilled with many nice illustrations and stories when describing the concepts, design and implementation of the YunFS. Wish you felt happy when reading this fully illustrated *technical* book.

Figure 0.2   It is a piece of cake to read this book.

YunFS is written in ANSI C, however, to clearly describe the flowchart of the complicated program, I use the JavaScript Language to write those pseudo codes. The advantage of using it is that the pseudo codes are much cleaner to read and can be understood easily.

HONGLIANG,ZHU

Sunnyvale, California
January, 2016

ACRONYMS

ERP   Enterprise resource planning (ERP) is a category of business-management softwaretypically a suite of integrated applicationsthat an organization can use to collect, store, manage and interpret data from many business activities, including: product planning, cost. manufacturing or service delivery. marketing and sales.

NoSQL   A NoSQL (originally referring to "non SQL" or "non relational") database provides a mechanism for storage and retrieval of data which is modeled in means other than the tabular relations used in relational databases.

IDL   IDL, short for Interactive Data Language, is a programming language used for data analysis. It is popular in particular areas of science, such as astronomy, atmospheric physics and medical imaging.

RPC   Remote Procedure Call (RPC) is a protocol that one program can use to request a service from a program located in another computer in a network without having to understand network details. (A procedure call is also sometimes known as a function call or a subroutine call.) RPC uses the client/server model.

SWIG   Swig. A simple, powerful, and extendable JavaScript Template Engine.

OSKIT   The OSKit is a framework and a set of 34 component libraries oriented to operating systems

COM   Component Object Model (COM) is a binary-interface standard for software components introduced

OSGI   The OSGi technology is a set of specifications that define a dynamic component system for Java.

ZFS   The Z File System, or ZFS , is an advanced file system designed to overcome many of the major problems found in previous designs. Originally developed at Sun, ongoing open source ZFS development has moved to the OpenZFS Project.

JSON   JSON (JavaScript Object Notation) is a lightweight data-interchange format. It is easy for humans to read and write. It is easy for machines to parse and generate.

BSON   BSON is a computer data interchange format used mainly as a data storage and network transfer format in the MongoDB database. It is a binary form for representing simple data structures and associative arrays (called objects or documents in MongoDB).

CLI   A command-line interface or command language interpreter (CLI), also known as command-line user interface, console user interface

PASOX   Paxos is a family of protocols for solving consensus in a network of unreliable processors. Consensus is the process of agreeing on one result among a group of participants. This problem becomes difficult when the participants or their communication medium may experience failures.

RAFT   Raft is a consensus algorithm designed as an alternative to Paxos. It was meant to be more understandable than Paxos by means of separation of logic, but it is also formally proven safe and offers some new features.

CHAPTER 1

INTRODUCTION

1.1   The Origin of YunFS

Yun is the cloud's Pinyin in Chinese, and my net name is 'yunhai', translated into English is Cloud Ocean. So I named this filesystem YunFS. In brief YunFS is a distributed filesystem based on the Cloud Storage.

Figure 1.1   YunFS Logo

About seven years ago, in 2009, at that time my girlfriend was working in a commercial business company. In the company, people used an ERP system to manage their orders, she always complaining about how hard is the ERP to use. To gain more likeness from her, I made a boast to her, "If you feel hard to use this ERP, I can write a new one for you, and if you like to use it, you can give it to your company." She was very happy when hearing that someone wish to develop a software especially for her and the most important is that, it is totally free. She said she would 100% support me to do this, so I began my journey of developing this ERP system.

Figure 1.2   Such a big boast!

I am a system programmer, I think an ERP system can be simply built by a NoSQL server and web GUI with some logic to manage the records, which is very easy and no challenge for me to do this, so I need make a challenge for myself. Shall I develop a new NoSQL server for this ERP system?

"Are you crazy? To develop an ERP system, you decide to develop a new NoSQL server?"

Of course your feeling is right, but at that time, I am not crazy, to keep improving the ability of computer programming, I always randomly put up some targets and regard it as a challenge.

Figure 1.3   Embarrassed

Figure 1.4   Think of reinventing a wheel

About a few months later, when I traveled with my girlfriend in a town with her company friends, at dinner time, her friend asked me: "I heard that you were developing an ERP system for us, how about the status of this ERP?" I took a weep smile and told her that:"I am making a big wheel, need more time to do this". Unfortunately, till now, I have not finished this ERP system, but she did not blame me for this. Though ERP is dead, YunFS is born. This is the story about YunFS's origin.

Figure 1.5 Marry me with YunFS

1.2 The Journey of YunFS

When I decide to develop a NoSQL server for ERP, I think that there is no big difference from the NoSQL and the filesystem. Comparing to the traditional filesystem, the NoSQL server is more popular in recent years with many more users. However, I am more familiar with the filesystem than NoSQL server, and filesystem seems more attractive to me. The most important is that filesystem can also provide powerful database to use, as in my original design this filesystem will not use the traditional filesystem concept but it is more like a full memory cache server. Due to it, so I decide to develop a new concept filesystem. This decision was made on the first day of beginning the journey of ERP.

At first, YunFS was named as SlabFS. If you are familiar with the Linux Kernel, you may know that the Slab is the key technical used to manage the memory. With the Solaris' ZFS coming to the world, the ZFS gives the world a deep impression, the disk management can be treated as memory management, there is no volume concept, but replace it by using the pool. When I took a source insight study with the ZFS, I thought, the disk management should be completely treated as memory management. This new design filesystem should be more radical and more pure than ZFS, because the File management is treated as Memory management, the disk block management also adopts memory techniques. The slab is a good choice, it already proved that was very suitable for small tricky memory blocks. So the full memory operational filesystem is YunFS' first feature, it is a liner address memory block that all the disk blocks are treated as.

With the popularity of the Cloud Computing and Cloud Storage, the solo machine's filesystems are losing their focus from the public. So when the first prototype of SlabFS finished, I meet my first question is what's the meaning of the SlabFS? There are so many local disk filesystems in the world, nothing missing without the SlabFS. So I took a deep thinking of SlabFS' future, it should become a distributed filesystem which was based on the Cloud Storage. Why need we base on a Cloud Storage? Because the Cloud Storage is an object filesystem, it is a distributed hash key-value filesystem. The object filesystem does not have the directory layer concept. The distributed key&value concept is its most important feature. So I renamed the SlabFS YunFS which was a distributed filesystem based on Cloud storage.

As a distributed filesystem, the biggest challenge is the distributed data consistence issue. To resolve this issue we adopt the RAFT protocol to keep the distributed data consistency. To put simply, the RAFT protocol is a leader's responsibility. It is only the leader who has the right to write, all other followers just can read. The leader is voted by the followers, a follower is also a candidate who has the possibility to become a leader.

To save the cost of using Cloud Storage, we stored one or two compressed copies to the Cloud Storage, and the data cached on the local disk is requested by demand. The distributed meta-data stored in each YunFS' node are about the piece block's version number and hash value. With the synchronization of distributed piece version and hash, the YunFS' node can get notified by every block's modification, if they have cached the blocks in local disk, they would request the remote Cloud Storage to refresh modified piece blocks immediately.

With more and more people begin to use Bitcoin in their real life, the distributed block chain concept brings me some ideas. The YunFS adopts the Bitcoin's block chain concept in its design, the disk block is spliced into many small pieces of blocks with fixed size, and those blocks are stored in the Cloud Storage like S3 or other popular Cloud Storage. Supported by more Disk Modules, the disk blocks can be stored in any other Cloud Storage. The YunFS' largest disk support size is 2^{64} byte, which is enough to use even an unlimited storage size announced by the Cloud Storage

Company. The YunFS' design philosophy is large enough to use. However, I don't want to speak it is unlimited, because we just use very small size.

1.3   Brief Description Of YunFS

As a cloud based distributed filesystem, YunFS has some different features from the traditional filesystem, YunFS' disk blocks are directly stored on the Cloud Storage, there is no volume concept, and using a very large liner storage which are spliced into many small chain blocks. Cloud Storage announced that it provides a high availability and stability with its service of 99.999%, the YunFS can be benefit from the stable service of the Cloud Storage. We don't need concern about the damage, nor lost blocks. If the service can't provide stability of one Cloud Storage, we can store a copy in another Cloud Storage, that is a double safety guarantee of the data.

- Based on a distributed framework, the RPC is a default feature. So a follower can directly have a remote call to the leader to obtain some privilege service like as create/delete/add/remove.

- The framework provides complete dynamic and modular design, it is easy to install, remove, start, stop a module with the CLI interface. You can see every module's current status, whether it is in running or stopped.

- The framework provides an automatic code generator. With an IDL file, you can easily develop a new module for YunFS, all necessary files are automatically generated in seconds. In the other word, when you finished the IDL file you will see the running result within seconds.

- It is a filesystem who can provide directory concept and streaming read&write, the AWS S3 Cloud Storage has not ability to provide them. I will explain why YunFS can do it in following chapters.

- As a full memory operational filesystem, the disk blocks are treated as memorys to be managed. All the blocks which exist on disk shall also have caches in memory at the same time. All the operations will be finished in memory at first, then sync dirty data to disk in scheduled time.

- Adopting the Bitcoin's block chain concept, the large liner disk storage is split into many small pieces of files. It is unnecessary to request for getting or putting a very large file to Cloud Storage, and this request is scheduled by demand.

- Provide RESTful service to the YunFS, it is simple for any other third online service to access the YunFS. The RESTful service can create, add, remove, read and write files.

- Distributed data consistence, YunFS is a one-leader-and-many-followers design, the distributed algorithm is RAFT. Only the leader has the read, write, add and remove privilege, and a follower just has the read right. Because followers are isolated from each other in design, they don't have the dependence relation, the performance can be scaled as line rate, The more followers, the better a read performance can be. To deploy YunFS follower as nearest location policy, the end-user can be benefit from the nearest location service, this is attractive for some based location service.

Ha, ha, this is the architecture of YunFS, built by those ten modules.

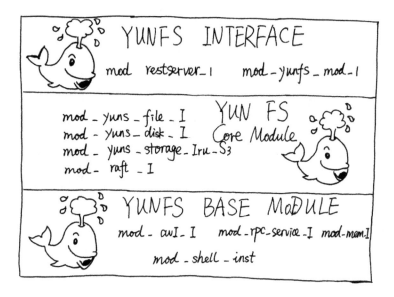

Figure 1.6 YunFS Architecture

Let's run the `ps` command in YunFS' CLI console, you will find ten modules installed and running as active status.

```
1  help ps install uninstall start stop show run
2  --->ps
3  1 mod_shell_inst active
4  2 mod_rpc_service_I active
5  3 mod_avl_II active
6  4 mod_mem_I active
7  5 mod_raft_I active
8  6 mod_yunfs_storage_III_raft_lru_s3 active
9  7 mod_yunfs_disk_I active
10 8 mod_yunfs_file_I active
11 9 mod_yunfs_cmd_I active
12 10 mod_restserver_I active
```

Listing 1.1 ps

CHAPTER 2

DISTRIBUTED FRAMEWORK

To do a good job, must first sharpen his device.

—Confucius

2.1 History Of Evolution

Why I develop this distributed framework? To answer this question, I would at first list some pains when developing a large system. A system consists of many modules, each module has its own interface functions, then modules can communicate with each other from their interface functions. This is a standard way in system design. However, with the interface function provided by module takes some modification or update, the interface function compatible issue will happen, other modules who call this upgraded interface function will report compile warning or error. If someone unfortunately missed this warning, the system may crash in further, because there is no version control with the interface functions. If one module takes a fresh update, in the normal way, this module need take recompile and combined statically together with the main program, unless the main process support plugin modules, and likely this module is a plugin module. While, in most system designs, core modules are usually statically linked together, only third plugin module support dynamic loading. The module does not have its own status, like running, stopped, or loaded status, so there is no way to hot plug module with active running program.

We usually undertake the pains in system design, to overcome those pains, we keep the module independent and object class are introduced in system design, even object class has its own issues. The inheritance and polymorphisms of object class may cause the module complex and virus infection from some instability base class. In modern factory, module encapsulation design has already been proven its value in system design.

Figure 2.1 Lego

Let us take a review with this Distributed Framework's history of evolution, the development of system is always a polishing procedure. And as the procedure was kept polishing, the evolution happens, new feature is added or some out of date features are abandoned, this can be concluded as spiral development. The origin thought of developing this framework comes from OSKIT, which is a component based operation system. When studying this OSKIT many years ago, I was deeply impressed by its component design. There are many components can be freely organized together by glue codes like Lego. I like this Lego like modular design, so I write this framework.

Figure 2.2   YunFS is compounded by several Lego modules

Though this component framework is very useful, it is a hard work to use it in a real project, there are so many glue codes like defining headers, interface source files, I have to write all these glue codes by hand. It is always a pain for me to use this component framework. The Ruby, Rails framework brings me some ideas. As a modern framework, the Ruby, Rails framework can generate code automatically, in one world "Don't waste your time repeating it again". So I decide to design an IDL language, with IDL language a user can define the Interface function, the framework will firstly parse the IDL language, then can automatically generate all the necessary glue codes. This IDL language is the subset of C Language. The User doesn't need to waste his time to learn a new Interface language. The generator is written by Shell script, with the parameter input to the Shell, and will generate all glue codes.

With the help of Shell and IDL, the generator can automatically produce glue codes. Because of the Shell language' limitation, it is not easy to create a new generator. At this time, it becomes necessary to introduce template concept to the framework, and the JavaScript language proved itself to be the most powerful and popular script language in the world. JavaScript has much more scalability than the Shell language. So I introduced a JavaScript template engine SWIG to this Distributed Framework. The IDL parser will output the JSON files firstly, then template engine SWIG will translate the JSON file into the target files by using the template. With this template engine, the framework can easily enlarge its capability to satisfy new requirement of generating different glue codes.

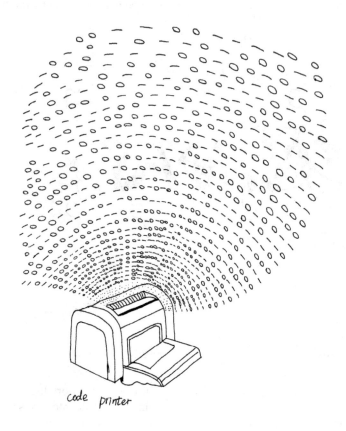

Figure 2.3   Code printer

If you are using the Java language to build up a large system, you may ever hear the OSGI Framework, which can dynamically list service's status and loads or remove the service. Of course, this good dynamically hot-plug feature is included in this framework. With plug easy modular design, we can easily replace a wrong module by a correct one.

During the development of YunFS, the target has been changed from the local filesystem to a distributed filesystem. RPC is imported into this framework, with the RPC, no matter where are the modules located, it can communicate with each other. The data structure encapsulated in RPC need to be defined, there are many choices for this data structure, enclosure, from Binary to String, for an example, the ASN.1, BSON is binary, JSON and XML is a string. This was an important decision to choose the data structure encapsulate, I selected the JSON. Why I did not use Binary? I think, with JSON, any other third program can directly call the RPC if they satisfy the JSON spec. JSON is readable string, it is very helpful in debugging and transition. Binary encapsulate may be better in performance, MongoDB use the BSON a binary JSON as its remote call encapsulate. It is a trade off decision to select JSON for the benefit of readable data structure encapsulate.

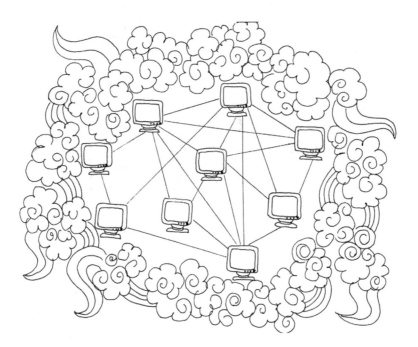

Figure 2.4   Communication by network

2.2   The Concept of the Distributed Framework

Take a brief description with those concepts in advance.

- Module
  The Module defines common Interface Functions, for example, you want to create a memory module, which defines the *malloc( )* and *free( )* interface functions. Modules can communicate with each other by Interface Function.

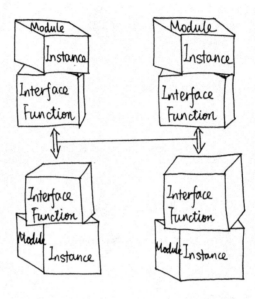

Figure 2.5   Modules communicate with each other by interface

- Instance

  The instance is the real implementation of the module. We can create several instances of a module with complete different implementations. Take the memory module as an example, one instance is named `mod_mem_I` that adapts glibc's allocation implementation, another instance is named `mod_mem_II` that adapts Slab's allocation implementation. You can switch to use them dynamically.

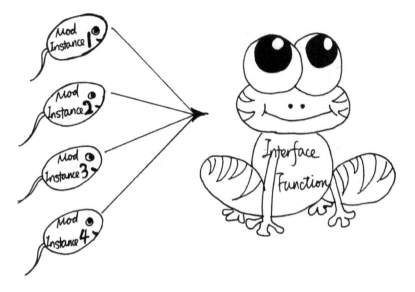

Figure 2.6 Mother Frog, many child tadpoles.

Adopting the instance is helpful when in development and deployment. In the process of development, if you want to adopt a new technique to take a rewrite, you can remain the old instance and create a new one that adopts the new technique. Also in the process of deploying, if an instance meets some wrong situation, you can uninstall this broken instance, and quickly install another with a new correct instance, the system will recover to normal in seconds.

Figure 2.7 Replace broken tire.

2.3   A Sample Module

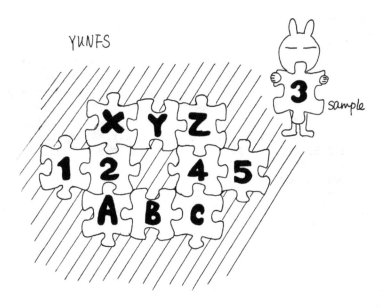

Figure 2.8   Sample Module.

2.3.1   Sample IDL File

The IDL language is the subset of the C language, you can write code in C, below is a sample demo IDL file.

In the first line, it defines the module name, and the instance name in the 2nd line. I usually use the Roman number like I, II, III, IV to note instance number, we can also choose another meaningful name to clarify different instances. Following is Interface Function, all interface functions should be defined in this IDL file.

```
1   #define MODULE "mod_demo"
2   #define INSTANCE "mod_demo_I"
3
4   int hello_world(char *str);
```

Listing 2.1   mod_demo_I

2.3.2 Generate Target Files

Run command 'auto_create' to generate target files automatically with predefined
IDL file.

```
1  # ./auto_create IDL/mod_demo_I.idl
2  STATE START
3  STATE CREATE JSON
4  output {"module":"mod_demo","instance":"mod_demo_I","
      defines":[],"structs":[],"methods":[{"ret":{"type":"
      TYPE_INT","ptr_struct":""},"name":"hello_world","args
      ":[{"type":"TYPE_PTR_CHAR","name":"str","ptr_struct
      ":""}]}],"IID":"0x04b13c5e, 0xf63d, 0xf464, 0x6f, 0xf0,
       0x14, 0x2d, 0x12, 0x6e, 0xf0, 0x47","SID":"0xe90b25a8,
       0x7f75, 0x5532, 0x16, 0x1d, 0x89, 0x87, 0xcb, 0xab, 0
      x00, 0xc0"}
5  STATE CREATE PATCH
6  STATE MKDIR
7  mkdir mod_demo_I
8  STATE PUB_INC_DESC
9  STATE PUB_INC_H
10 STATE PRI_INC_INST_H
11 STATE PRI_SRC_INST_C
12 STATE PRI_SRC_BUNDLE_C
13 STATE PRI_SRC_MAKEFILE
14 STATE PRI_SRC_STUB_SHELL
15 STATE PRI_SRC_STUB_RPC
16 STATE PRI_SRC_STUB_RPC_CALL
17 STATE APPLY_PATCH
18 STATE FINISH
```

Listing 2.2   auto_create

The generated target files include header, source, shell stub and RPC stub files.
All those files will be used in the Distributed Component Framework. You don't need
to hand write those files, but just putting a simple *run* command. I agree with the
Ruby on Rails's words,"Don't waste your time to repeat it again". This Distributed
Component Framework will help you finish those dirty things.

```
1  ./mod_demo_I
2  ./mod_demo_I/public
3  ./mod_demo_I/public/include
4  ./mod_demo_I/public/include/mod_demo.h
5  ./mod_demo_I/public/include/desc
6  ./mod_demo_I/private
```

```
7   ./mod_demo_I/private/include
8   ./mod_demo_I/private/include/mod_demo_I.h
9   ./mod_demo_I/private/src
10  ./mod_demo_I/private/src/mod_demo_I_bundle.c
11  ./mod_demo_I/private/src/stub
12  ./mod_demo_I/private/src/stub/stub_rpc_mod_demo_I.c
13  ./mod_demo_I/private/src/stub/stub_shell_mod_demo_I.c
14  ./mod_demo_I/private/src/stub/stub_rpc_mod_demo_I_call.c
15  ./mod_demo_I/private/src/mod_demo_I.c
16  ./mod_demo_I/private/src/makefile
```

2.4   Internal Implementation Of Sample Module

This section will begin to explain the internal implementation of module, to better understand the concept, we use above demo module as an example.

2.4.1   Header Files of the Sample Module

mod_demo_I/public/include/mod_demo.h

The following file `/mod_demo_I/public/include/mod_demo.h` is generated by the framework's code generator. Looking inside the source codes, we can see the file defined a COM alike structure with three basic functions, *mod_demo_query()*, *mod_demo_addref()* and *mod_demo_release()*. With those three interface functions, any other modules can access this demo module instance by calling *mod_demo_query()* function, no need to know its concrete instance ID.

To start or stop the instance, we defined *mod_demo_init()* and *mod_demo_cleanup()* functions, which will be called at the time when we started or stopped the instance.

The interface functions are included *mod_demo_hello_world()* and *rpc_demo_hello_world()*, any other modules can call those functions to access the instance of demo module.

```
1   #ifndef MOD_DEMO_H
2   #define MOD_DEMO_H
3
4
5   #include "mod.h"
6   #include "stl_common.h"
7
8
9   /*******************************************************
10  *                                                     *
11  *                    Define                           *
12  *                                                     *
13  *******************************************************/
14
```

```
15
16  /***struct_define***/
17
18
19  /***macro_define***/
20
21
22  /*******************************************************
23   *                                                     *
24   *                    COM Define                       *
25   *                                                     *
26   *******************************************************/
27
28
29  typedef struct mod_demo_st {
30          struct mod_demo_ops_st *p_ops;
31          stl_int_t ref_count;
32  } mod_demo_t;
33
34
35  struct mod_demo_ops_st {
36          MOD_IUNKNOWN(mod_demo_t);
37          stl_int_t(*init) (mod_demo_t * m);
38          stl_int_t(*cleanup) (mod_demo_t * m);
39  /***func_define***/
40          stl_int_t(*hello_world) (mod_demo_t * m, stl_char_t
                  * str);
41
42
43          stl_int_t
44                  (*rpc_hello_world) (mod_demo_t * m, stl_char_t
                      * remote_ip,
45                                      stl_int_t remote_port,
                                          stl_char_t * str);
46
47
48  };
49
50  /*******************************************************
51   *                                                     *
52   *                   Global Variable                   *
53   *                                                     *
54   *******************************************************/
55  #define MOD_DEMO_IID MOD_GUID(0x04b13c5e, 0xf63d, 0xf464, 0
          x6f, 0xf0, 0x14, 0x2d, 0x12, 0x6e, 0xf0, 0x47)
56  #define MOD_DEMO "mod_demo"
57
58
59  extern struct mod_guid_st mod_demo_iid;
```

```
60
61
62   /****************************************************
63    *                                                *
64    *                Interface Function              *
65    *                                                *
66    ****************************************************/
67   #define mod_demo_query(m, iid, out_ihandle) ((m)->p_ops->
         query((mod_demo_t *)(m), (iid), (out_ihandle)))
68   #define mod_demo_addref(m) ((m)->p_ops->addref((mod_demo_t
         *)(m)))
69   #define mod_demo_release(m) ((m)->p_ops->release((
         mod_demo_t *)(m)))
70   #define mod_demo_init(m) ((m)->p_ops->init((mod_demo_t *)(m
         )))
71   #define mod_demo_cleanup(m) ((m)->p_ops->cleanup((
         mod_demo_t *)(m)))
72
73
74   /***interface_define***/
75   #define mod_demo_hello_world(m,str) ((m)->p_ops->
         hello_world((mod_demo_t *)m,str))
76
77
78   #define rpc_mod_demo_hello_world(m, r, p,str) ((m)->p_ops->
         rpc_hello_world((mod_demo_t *)m, r, p,str))
79
80
81   #endif
```

Listing 2.3   mod_demo.h

2.4.2   Source Files of the Sample Module

mode_demo_I/private/src/mod_demo_I.c

Following file is also generated by the framework's code generator, which includes implementation functions of an instance of demo module. If a module needs to take some initiation at startup or some cleanup at destroy, you can add codes in *mod_demo_I_init()*, *mod_demo_I_cleanup()*.

The *mod_demo_hello_world()* function is the place to add some meaningful codes, in this sample module, we add some print codes in this function. All other functions, please leave as it is, don't try to modify it.

```
1
2   #include "mod_demo_I.h"
3
4
```

```
5   struct mod_guid_st mod_demo_I_sid = MOD_DEMO_I_SID;
6
7
8   stl_int_t
9   RPC_CLIENT_mod_demo_I_hello_world(stl_char_t * remote_ip,
        stl_int_t remote_port,
10                                        stl_char_t * str);
11
12
13  stl_int_t mod_demo_I_query(IN mod_demo_t * p_m,
14                            IN mod_iid_t * iid, OUT
                               stl_void_t ** out_ihandle)
15  {
16          if (memcmp(iid, &mod_iunknown_iid, sizeof(*iid)) ==
                0 ||
17             memcmp(iid, &mod_demo_iid, sizeof(*iid)) == 0)
                    {
18                  *out_ihandle = p_m;
19                  mod_demo_addref(p_m);
20                  return 0;
21          }
22
23
24          *out_ihandle = 0;
25          return -1;
26  };
27
28
29  stl_uint_t mod_demo_I_addref(mod_demo_t * p_m)
30  {
31          return ++p_m->ref_count;
32  }
33
34
35  stl_uint_t mod_demo_I_release(mod_demo_t * p_m)
36  {
37          if (--p_m->ref_count) {
38                  return 0;
39          }
40          FREE(p_m);
41          return 0;
42  }
43
44  stl_int_t mod_demo_I_init(mod_demo_t * p_m)
45  {
46          return 0;
47  }
48
49
```

```
50  stl_int_t mod_demo_I_cleanup(mod_demo_t * p_m)
51  {
52          return 0;
53  }
54
55
56  /***func_implemation***/
57
58
59  stl_int_t mod_demo_I_hello_world(mod_demo_t * m, stl_char_t
        * str)
60  {
61          stl_printf("###%s str:%s###\n", __FUNCTION__, str);
62          return 0;
63  }
64
65
66  stl_int_t
67  mod_demo_I_rpc_hello_world(mod_demo_t * m, stl_char_t *
        remote_ip,
68                              stl_int_t remote_port,
                                    stl_char_t * str)
69  {
70          return RPC_CLIENT_mod_demo_I_hello_world(remote_ip,
                remote_port, str);
71  }
72
73
74  struct mod_demo_ops_st mod_demo_I_ops = {
75          mod_demo_I_query,
76          mod_demo_I_addref,
77          mod_demo_I_release,
78          mod_demo_I_init,
79          mod_demo_I_cleanup,
80          /***func_ops***/
81          mod_demo_I_hello_world,
82
83
84          mod_demo_I_rpc_hello_world
85  };
86
87  stl_int_t mod_demo_I_create_instance(mod_iid_t * p_iid,
        mod_iid_t * p_sid,
88                                          stl_void_t **
                                            pp_ihandle)
89  {
90          mod_demo_t *p_m = NULL;
91
92
```

```
93              p_m = (mod_demo_t *) CALLOC(1, sizeof(mod_demo_t));
94              p_m->p_ops = &mod_demo_I_ops;
95
96
97              return mod_demo_query(p_m, p_iid, pp_ihandle);
98      }
```

2.4.3   Stub Files of the Sample Module

It's necessary for the Distributed Component Framework to use below files to support dynamic module load/unload, script and RPC. In those files, the data structure will be translated into a JSON string. For example *demo_hello_world(char *str)*'s input parameter `str` will be translated into a JSON string `{"str":"hello world"}`. We can find soon in the next chapters that the complex data structure is also supported. The RPC stubs are also included and which are used to support Remote Process Call feature in distributed systems.

- private/src/mod_demo_I_bundle.c

- private/src/stub/stub_rpc_mod_demo_I.c

- private/src/stub/stub_rpc_mod_demo_I_call.c

- private/src/stub/stub_shell_mod_demo_I.c

2.4.4   How To Access the Sample Module

If we want to call interface functions of an instance of demo module, we should follow below steps so.

- Get the SID of module service and then query to get one instance of the module.

- Call the interface function, in this sample code *mod_demo_hello_world ()*.

- Don't forget to release the service and instance.

```
1   #include "mod_demo.h"
2
3
4   int call_demo_hello_world()
5   {
6           mod_iid_t *mod_sid;
7           mod_demo_t *m;
8
9
10          STL_VASSERT((mod_sid = (struct mod_guid_st *)
11              mod_bundle_service_get(MOD_DEMO)) != NULL);
```

```
12
13
14        STL_VASSERT(mod_query_instance(mod_sid,
15            (stl_void_t **) & m) == STL_RV_SUC);
16
17
18        mod_demo_hello_world(m, "hello world");
19
20        mod_bundle_service_put(MOD_DEMO);
21        mod_release_instance(m);
22  }
```

2.5   The Internal Implementation of Distributed Component Framework

2.5.1   The CLI of Distributed Component Framework

The CLI service of the framework is provided by `mod_shell_Int`, it is an instance of the Shell module which is installed with the framework. The `mod_shell_int` provides a very simple script mode to let users install, uninstall, start, stop, show, run with an instance of the module.

- show
  Display installed instance's information, dependence, etc., you can manually modify the mod_demo_I/public/include/desc file to change the instance's description.

- ps
  Display installed instance's status, the installed means the instance is installed, instead of in running status. The active means the instance is running.

- run
  To call the interface function, the following parameter is a JSON string that is used to pass the parameter to interface function.

- install
  To install an instance of the module. If an instance is installed, you can type `ps` to watch its status is in `installed` status.

- uninstall
  To uninstall an instance of the module. If an instance is uninstalled, it will be destroyed. Type `ps` will not see this instance's information.

- start
  After installing an instance of a module, it is time to start this instance, if the instance is successfully started, the status will be in `active` status.

- stop
  To stop running the active instance.

- help
  Display help information.

Right now, the CLI of framework is simple and provided with the above commands.

```
1  root@localhost:/tmp/deploy# ./yunfs
2  help ps install uninstall start stop show run
3
4
5  --->ps
6     1 mod_shell_inst          active
7     2 mod_rpc_service_I       active
8     3 mod_demo_I              active
9
10
11 --->show 3
12
13
14 {
15    "name":"mod_demo",
16    "description": "",
17    "version": "0.0.1",
18    "author": "author",
19    "dependence":{
20       "mod_shell":"0.0.1"
21    },
22    "interface":[
23
24
25    ]
26 }
27 --->run mod_demo_hello_world {"str":"hello world, welcome
      to framework"}
28 function mod_demo_hello_world args {"str":"hello world,
      welcome to framework"}
29
30
31 ###mod_demo_I_hello_world str:hello world, welcome to
      framework###
32
33
34 { "response": { "ret": { "ret": 0 } } }
35
36
37 --->
```

2.5.2 Install & Uninstall

The cmd `install` is the way to add a new created module into the Distributed Component Framework, while uninstall will remove the module from this framework. The module is compiled and linked as a dynamic library, the flowchart of the `install` & `uninstall` is listed below.

Figure 2.9 Install to table

- `Install` will register the bundle service of module by calling *mod_bundle_cmd_register()*, then calling *dlopen()* to load this dynamic library into the program. After the instance of the module is created by calling *mod_xxx_I_bundle_create_instance()*. There is an entry to be added into hash table where the query service can obtain the handle of a new created instance of the module.

- uninstall does the opposite things as install has done.

2.5.3   Start & Stop

With previous install cmd, a new created module is installed into the framework and its status is 'installed'. This start cmd will start the instance into active status. It will call *bundle_start()* function, which will register the interface functions to CLI module and RPC module. After registering to the CLI and RPC module, you can add some initialization with the instance in *mod_xxx_I_init()* function.

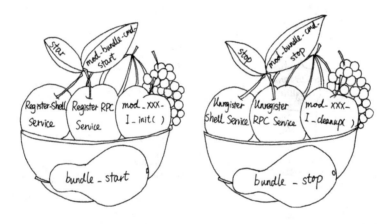

Figure 2.10   call to start or stop

- The new created instance, will register its service with CLI service and RPC service, so that we can run call and *RPC_call* to access the interface function of the module.

2.5.4   GetService & PutService

The Get-and-Put service is only provided by the API, with those API, you can get the handle of the instance. Right now, only the first one instance, will be queried from the Get Service. Don't try to install more instances with the same module, though the framework support one module and multiple instances. I would not suggest to `install` more instances, because the module management is complex, the dependence, conflict issue is the basement issue that all the module management would resolve. And `install` more instance does not help the modular of the program, but bring any troubles to the clearance of the system. We suggest only installing necessary modules, and uninstalling unused module, so that it can keep the whole system clean. I would like to present an example to prove this suggestion is correct, NodeJS's npm is the good example. We have experienced too much troublesome after introducing flexible configuration into system design, sometimes if taking some limitation with flexible configurations, we can gain more robust in system running. This is trade off in system design.

Figure 2.11   Get service

2.5.5 Call Interface Function

In order to debug a module with more test cases, the framework provides `run` command, by using `run` that can directly call the interface functions of the module at shell mode. The parameters of interface function should be manually fulfilled as a JSON string.

When module received the request JSON string, it will parse this JSON string into a data structure, then pass this data structure to the function call. The shell stubs of module did the parse work to translate data structure into JSON string or from JSON string back into a data structure.

The advantage of this design is that all the communication interface is driven by JSON, and any other third modules can call the interface functions of module if they follow the JSON spec. You can use any other languages, like JavaScript, Ruby, Python, C++ etc...

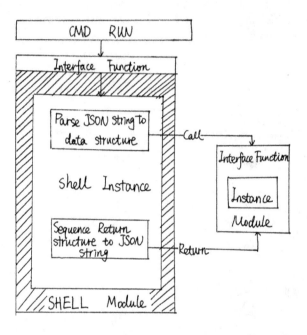

Figure 2.12   Run the command in CLI shell mode of Framework

Below is how the drawing in the CLI mode to call RPC with remote module. At first it passes to the Shell Module and call the XXX module to send out RPC request. In the other side, the RPC service receives RPC Request, takes a parse from the JSON string back into the data structure and then calls the XXX module's interface function, thus this is the RPC's main working flow.

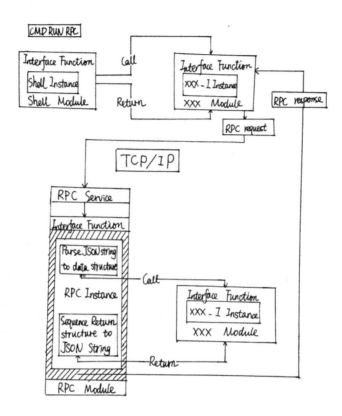

Figure 2.13   RPC working flow

CHAPTER 3

THE RESTFUL INTERFACE MODULE

3.1   Brief Description of the RESTful Interface

It is necessary for a cloud filesystem to provide a RESTful API for end-users who would like to access the YunFS. This RESTful provides LIST, GET, PUT, ADD and DEL service.

- LIST is used to display files in a directory.

- ADD is used to create a new directory.

- DEL is used to delete a directory or file.

- PUT is used to upload content to a new file with an absolute path.

- GET is used to get the content of a file by giving an absolute path. It supports offset seeking, which is very useful when playing with streaming video.

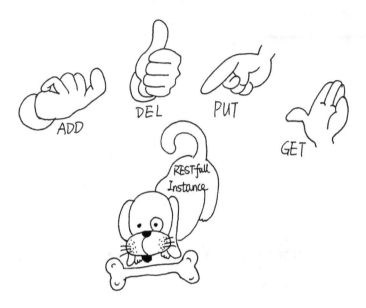

Figure 3.1   The Architecture of RESTful Module

With the same function as the shell mode, this RESTful Interface is also another official way to access the YunFS. Because YunFS is specifically designed for cloud web usage, it does not provide POSIX standard APIs for the end user.

The reason why chooses RESTful but not POSIX is that RESTful has been hot in recent years with the Cloud Computing keeping popular in the world. SIMPLE is RESTful's first tag. It does not take too much time to decide to adopt a RESTful interface as the only official interface to YunFS. Though the POSIX standard is useful for traditional filesystem, it is not helpful for the web usage. Background consideration, NFS is sinking, while the cloud object storage like AWS S3 begins to master the world, AWS S3 provides RESTful APIs as its only interface. It is a right decision with the RESTful API to keep up the steps of trending in Cloud Storage.

3.2   The Internal Design of the RESTful Interface

In this section, we will take a review with the design of RESTful Interface. The LIST, ADD, DEL, GET and PUT uses same working flow to handle corresponding HTTP request from user.

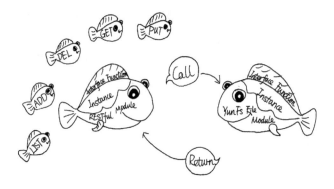

Figure 3.2   The LIST/ADD/DEL/GET/PUT Working Flow

- A client using browser to send out HTTP request that contains LIST, ADD, DEL, GET and PUT command.

- The RESTful interface module worked as a web server, it binds at a port to handle the HTTP request. We used a third HTTP server as its web server, this module's biggest target is to provide a wrapper layer to link the web server together.

- Real File functions are provided by the YunFS' File Module, so RESTful interface need call this YunFS' File Module to get correct information, then in response those data back to the client.

3.2.1 The Internal of LIST RESTful Interface

3.2.1.1 HTTP LIST Request and Response

```
1
2  Request URL: http://xxx.com:8001/RESTAPI/LIST?path=/
       DWmZdCvMADgkCpJg9
3  Request Method: POST
4  - Request Headers
5    Accept: */*
6    Accept-Encoding: gzip, deflate
7    Accept-Language: en-US, en; q=0.8, zh-Hans-CN; q=0.5, zh
       -Hans; q=0.3
8    Cache-Control: no-cache
9    Connection: Keep-Alive
10   Content-Length: 9
11   Content-Type: text/plain; charset=UTF-8
12   Host: xxx.com:8001
```

```
13     Referer: http://xxx.com:2001/list?path=/
           DWmZdCvMADgkCpJg9
14     User-Agent: Mozilla/5.0 (Windows NT 10.0) AppleWebKit
           /537.36 (KHTML, like Gecko) Chrome/42.0.2311.135
           Safari/537.36 Edge/12.10240
```

```
1
2  - Status Code: 200 / OK
3  - Response Headers
4    Access-Control-Allow-Origin: *
5    Content-Type: text/plain
6    Transfer-Encoding: chunked
7  - Response Body
8    [{"name":"a1", "type":"DIR", "size":0]
```

3.2.1.2 The Internal Implementation of HTTP LIST

Use JavaScript as pseudo code to describe the LIST working flow, it will be recursive to get all file lists of the current path and return data in JSON.

```
1
2  function handle_http(http)
3  {
4      if (http.type == "LIST"){
5          var dir;
6          var resp = [];
7
8          var path = parse_path_from_url(http.url);
9
10         if (check_path_exist(path) == false){
11             return resp;
12         }
13
14         while (dir = YunFS_readdir(path, dir)){
15           attr = yunfs_getattr(dir);
16
17           resp.add(
18             {
19               name:attr.name,
20               type:attr.type,
21               size:attr.size
22             });
23         }
24         return resp;
25     }
26  }
```

Listing 3.1   handle_http(http)

❹ Make sure the HTTP's request type is LIST and get the absolute path later from HTTP request's parameter.

❽ Check whether the path is valid or not, if not, it will return with null array.

⓮ Take a loop to obtain all files which are located in current path. *yunfs_readdir( )* is an interface function which is provided by YunFS's File Module to list all files of the current directory.

⓯ In this while loop, it will get not only the attribute of a file by calling *yunfs_getattr( )* but also the attribute includes the file's name, type and size.

⓱ Add every file's attribute name, type and size of the array, then return this JSON array to client.

3.2.2   The Internal of CREATE RESTful Interface

3.2.2.1   *HTTP CREATE Request and Response*

```
1
2  Request URL: http://xxx.com:8001/RESTAPI/CREATE?path=/
       X4LpEJdqCyDzvTimZ/d5
3  Request Method: GET
```

```
1
2  Status Code: 200 / OK
3     Request Headers
4   - Response Headers
5     Access-Control-Allow-Origin: *
6     Content-Type: text/plain
7     Transfer-Encoding: chunked
```

3.2.2.2   *Internal Implementation of CREATE*

CREATE is used to create a new directory or plain file from giving the absolute path.

```
1
2  function handle_http(http)
3  {
4     if (http.type == "CREATE"){
5        var resp = [];
6        var path = parse_path_from_url(http.url);
7
8     if (check_path_exist(path) == false){
9           return resp;
10        }
11
```

```
12          yunfs_create(path, "DIR");
13      }
14  }
```

Listing 3.2   handle_http(http)

❻ Parse the URL to get the path, then check this path is valid or not, if not return with null array.

❽ Check whether the path exists or not, if not, return with null array.

⓬ Call YunFS module to create a new directory by calling *yunfs_create()*.

3.2.3   The Internal of DELETE RESTful Interface

3.2.3.1   *HTTP DELETE Request and Response*

```
1
2  Request URL: http://yunhaia.com:8001/RESTAPI/DELETE?path=/
       X4LpEJdqCyDzvTimZ/d4
3      Request Method: GET
4      Status Code: 200 / OK
5      Request Headers
```

```
1
2  Status Code: 200 / OK
3  Response Headers
4
5      Access-Control-Allow-Origin: *
6      Content-Type: text/plain
7      Transfer-Encoding: chunked
```

3.2.3.2   *Internal Implementation of DELETE*
Call to delete the file or directory.

```
1
2  function handle_http(http)
3  {
4      if (http.type == "DELETE"){
5          var resp = [];
6          var path = parse_path_from_url(http.url);
7
8          if (check_path_exist(path) == false){
9              return resp;
10         }
11
12         yunfs_remove(path);
```

```
13        }
14    }
```

Listing 3.3   handle_http(http)

➏ Same as previous interface functions, parse `http.url` to get the absolute path of a file or directory, and check whether this path is valid or not.

➓ Call the interface function of File Module *yunfs_remove( )* to remove file or directory by giving the absolute path.

3.2.4   The Internal Of PUT RESTful Interface

3.2.4.1   HTTP PUT Request and Response

```
1
2    Request URL: http://xxx.com:8001/RESTAPI/PUT?path=/
        X4LpEJdqCyDzvTimZ
3    Request Method: POST
4
5
6    - Request Headers
7    Accept: application/json
8    Accept-Encoding: gzip, deflate
9    Accept-Language: en-US, en; q=0.8, zh-Hans-CN; q=0.5, zh
        -Hans; q=0.3
10   Cache-Control: no-cache
11   Connection: Keep-Alive
12   Content-Length: 37041
13   Content-Type: multipart/form-data; boundary
        =-------------------------7df3d444c0584
14   Host: xxx.com:8001
15   Referer: http://xxx.com:2001/list?path=/
        X4LpEJdqCyDzvTimZ
16   User-Agent: Mozilla/5.0 (Windows NT 10.0) AppleWebKit
        /537.36 (KHTML, like Gecko) Chrome/42.0.2311.135
        Safari/537.36 Edge/12.10240
17   X-Requested-With: XMLHttpRequest
18
19
20   -------------------------7df3d444c0584
21   Content-Disposition: form-data; name="file"; filename="aa.
        pdf"
22   Content-Type: application/pdf
```

```
1
2    Status Code: 200 / OK
3    Response Headers
```

```
4    Access-Control-Allow-Headers: Cache-Control,X-Requested-
        With
5    Access-Control-Allow-Methods: *
6    Access-Control-Allow-Origin: *
7    Transfer-Encoding: chunked
```

3.2.4.2 *Internal Implementation of PUT*

Call the PUT to upload a file to YunFS, it will pare the HTTP request to get the `filename`, `type`, `data_length` and `context`, then to write the `context` to the file, if the file does not exist yet, it will create this file at first.

```
1
2    function handle_http(http)
3    {
4        if (http.type == "PUT"){
5            var path = parse_path_from_http(http);
6            var filename = parse_filename_from_http(http);
7            var fullpath = path + "/" + filename;
8            var data_len = parse_datalen_from_http(http);
9            var context = parse_data_from_http(http);
10
11           if (check_path_exist(fullpath) == false){
12               YunFS_create(fullpath, "FILE");
13           }
14
15           YunFS_write(fullpath, context, 0, data_len);
16       }
17   }
```

Listing 3.4 handle_http(http)

❺ Get the path from the Request URL: http://xxx.com:8001/RESTAPI/PUT?path=/X4LpEJdqCyDzvTimZ

❻ Get the `filename` from the Content-Disposition of http. form-data; name="file"; filename="aa.pdf"

❼ Combine the `fullpath` of file that is /X4LpEJdqCyDzvTimZ/aa.pdf

❽ Get length from Content-Length: 37041

❾ Parse to get the context of file from the HTTP Content-Type: multipart/form-data;

⓫ Check the path already exist or not, if not, it will create a new file.

⓯ Call the YunFS File module's interface function *yunfs_write()* to write the file with content.

3.2.5 The Internal Of GET RESTFul Interface

3.2.5.1   HTTP GET Request and Response

```
1
2  Request URL: http://xxx.com:8001/RESTAPI/GET?path=/
      X4LpEJdqCyDzvTimZ/aa.pdf&iframe=true&width=100%&height
      =100%
3  Request Method: GET
4  Request Headers
5  Accept: text/html, application/xhtml+xml, image/jxr, */*
6  Accept-Encoding: gzip, deflate
7  Accept-Language: en-US, en; q=0.8, zh-Hans-CN; q=0.5, zh-
      Hans; q=0.3
8  Connection: Keep-Alive
9  Host: yunhaia.com:8001
10 Referer: http://xxx.com:2001/list?path=/X4LpEJdqCyDzvTimZ
11 User-Agent: Mozilla/5.0 (Windows NT 10.0) AppleWebKit
      /537.36 (KHTML, like Gecko) Chrome/42.0.2311.135 Safari
      /537.36 Edge/12.10240
```

```
1
2  Status Code: 200 / OK
3    Response Headers
4    Accept-Ranges: bytes
5    Access-Control-Allow-Origin: *
6    Connection: keep-alive
7    Content-Disposition: inline; filename="aa.pdf"
8    Content-Length: 36852
9    Content-Type: application/pdf
10   Date: Thu, 24 Sep 2015 05:10:03 GMT
11   Etag: "560385ab.36852"
12   Last-Modified: Thu, 24 Sep 2015 05:10:03 GMT
```

```
1
2  Request URL: http://xxx.com:8001/RESTAPI/GET?path=/
      X4LpEJdqCyDzvTimZ/aa.pdf&iframe=true&width=100%&height
      =100%
3    Request Method: GET
4    Request Headers
5    Accept: */*
6    Accept-Encoding: gzip, deflate
7    Connection: Keep-Alive
8    GetContentFeatures.DLNA.ORG: 1
9    Host: xxx.com:8001
10   If-Range: "560385ab.36852"
11   Range: bytes=5534-
```

```
12   User-Agent: Mozilla/5.0 (Windows NT 10.0) AppleWebKit
        /537.36 (KHTML, like Gecko) Chrome/42.0.2311.135
        Safari/537.36 Edge/12.10240
```

```
1
2  Status Code: 206 / Partial Content
3     Response Headers
4     Accept-Ranges: bytes
5     Access-Control-Allow-Origin: *
6     Connection: keep-alive
7     Content-Disposition: inline; filename="aa.pdf"
8     Content-Length: 31318
9     Content-Range: bytes 5534-36851/36852
10    Content-Type: application/pdf
11    Date: Thu, 24 Sep 2015 05:10:03 GMT
12    Etag: "560385ab.36852"
13    Last-Modified: Thu, 24 Sep 2015 05:10:03 GMT
```

3.2.5.2 *The Internal Implementation of GET*

Get the content of a file by both giving the file's path and offset, and supporting HTTP range option to get streaming data of file.

```
1
2  function handle_http(http)
3  {
4     if (http.type == "GET"){
5        var fullpath = parse_path_from_http(http);
6
7        if (check_path_exist(fullpath) == false){
8           return;
9        }
10
11       var attr = YunFS_get_attr(fullpath);
12       var size = attr.size;
13
14       var offset = parse_range_from_http(http);
15       var read_size = YunFS_read(fullpath, context, offset,
              max_size);
16
17       FILL_HTTP_CONTEXT(context, offset, context, read_size
              );
18    }
19 }
```

Listing 3.5   handle_http(http)

❺ Parse the `fullpath` from Request URL:
http://xxx.com:8001/RESTAPI/GET?path=/X4LpEJdqCyDzvTimZ/aa.pdf

❼ Check the path is exist or not, if not, it will return.

⓬ Get the size of file with correct `fullpath` of the file.

⓮ Get the offset from the request of HTTP. Range: bytes=5534.

⓯ Call the YunFS File module's interface function *yunfs_read( )* to read the context of a file, the offset and size are the necessary input parameters.

⓱ Fill the context of file to HTTP's content, which will be returned to the HTTP client.

3.3   Conclusion of RESTful Interface

In this section, I introduced the internal implementation of RESTful interface. The RESTful itself is the evolution of Interface comparing to SOAP or other RPC interfaces. From the first time it comes into the world, more and more interfaces of Web Service have been provided by RESTful interface, besides on its SIMPLE feature, whose other advantage is that it is based on HTTP.

CHAPTER 4

THE FILE MODULE DESIGN

4.1   The Brief Description of the File Module

As mentioned in previous chapters, I firstly wanted to design a NoSQL database, but changed to design YunFS finally. A simple NoSQL database was almost similar to a hash table server, like Google's big-table. As well known as that, GFS, big-table and map-reduce were called Google's three papers, it was after Google released these three papers to the world that many people invent their own big-table by following Google's papers.

When I began to design the NoSQL database server, my first target is to build a big-table server. However, since the database was yet another filesystem, why not design directly a filesystem. And working with a filesystem, database base on it can do more things than its original capacity. After knowing that the mongoDB was developed at the top of GridFS I switched my target from a NoSQL big-table to a filesystem.

To design the File Module, I had to take a choice from the flat structure and the directory structure of file storage. During a distributed filesystem designing, most architectures would like to choose a flat structure and to drop the concept of a directory, it is because the directory concept is complex and dependence. A child directory need to be located under its parent directory. However, in a distributed system, simple, divide and conquer are the basic principle in its design. After dropping the concept of directories, a distributed filesystem won't need to take consideration of a recurring travel with directories, the full path is just a long unique string that contains some character '/' in it. There is no concept of a file's parent directory, all file's path is unique and equal in weight. Without those dependence, the distributed filesystem can be implemented and scaled easily.

Figure 4.1   Organized in the directory is cleaner than flat

YunFS still adopts the traditional filesystem's concept of the directory, which does have directory concept. The files are located in a directory, all files have a root directory /. Why I still designed YunFS in this way and did not follow traditional distributed filesystem's design. I think the directory is a good technique to keep files clear and organized. From a Library's book index with Web site's hypertext, the directory has already been proven its value of existence. A distributed filesystem drops the concept of directory because its drawback in its based on key-value design. Being given a key which is a file's full string path and been calculated with a distributed hash algorithm to obtain its value, then stores the key and value in storage at that time. Directory means nothing but a full path string to hash key.

In YunFS, File Module will manage directory and plain file. At this layer, they don't know where they stored, nor how they stored. File Module is concentrating its energy on file management of organized files and directories, at the same time leaving the distributed storage to be handled by Modules of Disk Management and LRU S3 Storage.

There are many file systems exist in the world, however, it is after ZFS comes to the world and gives a revelation that filesystem can be designed as a pool. The YunFS's File Module design is similar to ZFS, but much more simple. The YunFS's

Disk Object Management is not same as ZFS, but more like a memory management, and this Disk Module will be described in the next chapter.

YunFS is more like a modern filesystem. A global balanced tree is used to handle directory and it is cached in memory to speed up the searching. There are many reasons that YunFS dropped disk B+ tree in its design. When being added or removed items, a disk balanced tree had to take a balancing with its disk trees. So it needs take more modification with the disk nodes to keep the disk tree balanced, also searching in the disk balance tree needs access the low speed disk to find out the target. These two drawbacks, cost highly in disk storage. This is not an expected future of modern filesystem design. YunFS is regarded as a full memory operational filesystem, so the AVL tree does only exist in memory, but not in disk storage. All the operations like finding, adding, re-balancing are all operated in memory.

As a full memory operational filesystem, all the blocks which exist on disk shall also have caches in memory at the same time. All the operations were at first finished in memory, then at a scheduled time was triggered to synchronize dirty data from memory to disk. The reason why the design is in this way is that the memory will be cheaper and larger than before. Filesystem design should follow the rule of this to keep all things done in memory.

Figure 4.2   Running in memory is much faster than disk

YunFS works in his own way to drop the low speed disk and involve in a high speed memory. The operation of the disk is at a very low speed, so YunFS keeps the operating in high speed memory. Sometime at a critical time, if system crashed and the data stored in memory lost, the data would not sync with the disk. This condition will not affect the system. We adopt COW technical, Copy-On-Write, after using it a block if changed will copy a new one. On the other hand, if they did not take effect, they will still use the old one. Because of adopting all memory operations, the data stored on disk will be loaded as cache in memory, and the cache will remain temporarily until the next scheduled sync time arrived. Infos takes the use of a scheduled timeout task to do the synchronized work period, and this process is sporadic instead of real time.

4.2   The Internal Design and Implementation of the File Module

4.2.1   The Internal Data Structure Design

This section will introduce the internal data structure of directories and plain files, in this chapter, we can know how they are stored on disk. And in the next section will introduce how they are implemented.

4.2.1.1   Directory

- The `yunfs_dir_entry_t` structure defines a linked directory table which consists a 128-piece table `yunfs_dir_entry` and `next_ptr` which points to the next `yunfs_dir_entry_t` entry. With above diagram, we can know that the YunFS's directory is consisted by a linked entry table.

- Every `yunfs_dir_entry` is a 2^{64} integer number which points to a `yunfs_dir_attr_t` structure. This structure contains a name of a file or directory and the name's length is limited to 84 bytes. We don't suggest to give a file or directory a long name, because a 84 byte long string is enough to use. It is not necessary to support a very long and unlimited file name.

- The `block_id` in `yunfs_dir_attr_t` is also a 2^{64} integer number points to `yunfs_node_phys_t` structure, this structure is the key structure of the file.

- The first element `node_blockptr` is a structure of `yunfs_blockptr_t`, it points to the block's `offset`, `length` and `block_type` which is `BLOCK_TYPE_DATA`, `BLOCK_TYPE_BLOCKPTR_CHUNK` or `BLOCK_TYPE_DIR_LINK`.

- The `node_level` element describes which level of the current block's indirect block, more details of this element will be introduced in the next section.

- The `enum_node_type` describes that the current node is a plain file or a directory, or something others. Is it like a linked symbol? If you are familiar with Linux, Linux does have a hard or a soft link symbol which points to a directory or a file.

- The structure `yunfs_file_attr_t` describes the current file or directory's attribute which includes `size`, `birth`, `owner` and `block_size`. Noticed about this attribute `block_size`, YunFS dynamically calculates to determine a file's perfect `block_size` according to the file's actual size. It is a very important feature of YunFS that with correct `block_size` it can save the disk wastage and improve the performance of the file's reading or writing. Take a 1G file as an example, the file's `block_size` is 8M, it only has 128 blocks. With less blocks, the file's reading and writing can get a much better performance. Now, we again take a 10M file as an example, in traditional filesystem the file's `block_size` is a fixed number like 1k, so the 10M file has 1024*10 blocks. In the end, let's turn back to the 1G file example, the file's `block_size` is also 1k, it has 1024*1024 blocks, that is terrible. With the dynamic `block_size` calculation, we take a balance between the disk storage wastage and performance. Here, I want to exemplify Google's GFS, in GFS, the `block_size` of file is 64M, so they are more friendly with large files. However, this big 64M `block_size` is not suitable for small files, GFS has to chunk those small files together into a large file like zipping and take a internal index. In YunFS, we adopt dynamic `block_size` calculation, which is perfect for both small files and large files at the same time.

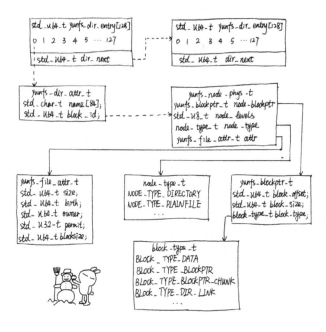

Figure 4.3   Directory structure I

Below is the real diagram which shows directory's recursive travel with deeper directories, there is no limitation to the directory's depth, and all directories share the Root as their common parent.

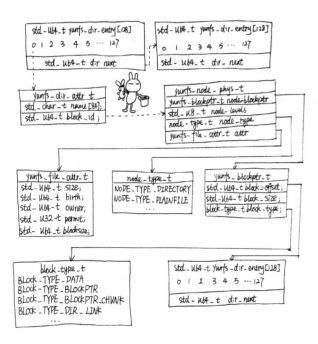

Figure 4.4   Directory structure II

4.2.1.2   Plain File

Below drawing shows the plain file contains some contents. The `node_type` is assigned as **NODE_TYPE_PLAINFILE** and `node_blockptr`'s `block_type` is assigned as **BLOCK_TYPE_BLOCKPTR_CHUNK**, it means that the `block_offset` points to a disk which is consist with a 24-element block-pointer table. By this way, I will introduce a very important concept of filesystem which is an indirect block. In filesystem designing, it is a basic implementation that manages the contents of a plain file. With Indirect block-pointers, the file's content are spliced into numerous blocks, each block has a fixed size. For example, if a block size is 512K and the file's size is 100M, we can simply calculate the number of blocks is $100 * 1024/512 = 200$. However, if we use indirect blocks we will have level 2's indirect blocks, $24 * 24 = 576$, and 200 is lower than 576, so the level of indirect block level is 2. The more indirect blocks, the more data can be contained, $24 * 24 * 24 * 24...$

As above mentioned the block's size is dynamically calculated by the size of real file, it is in order to take balance with the disk wastage and performance. The less indirect levels, the better performance can be. And it will cost less CPU time if with less recursive travel time of indirect blocks. The indirect block is a classic design in the filesystem, in YunFS, I take some improvements with the block chunk tables, assigning level 1 with 24 elements to replace 3 elements which are commonly used in the classic design of indirect blocks, it can avoid no enough level 1 elements to hold whole contents, so that we have to turn into level 2 and cost more time to travel with the indirect blocks.

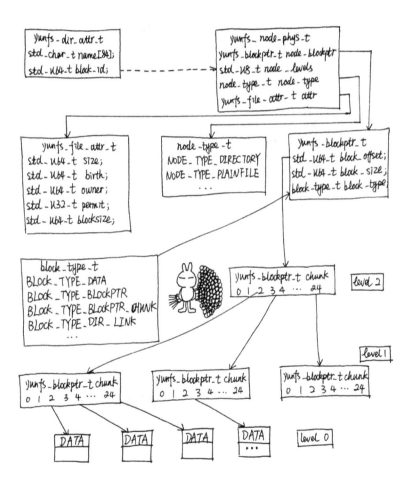

Figure 4.5   Plain file structure I

Below drawing describes the details of using DATA level 2, from it we find the chunk table points to the `disk_offset` which has a structure of `yunfs_blockptr`. This structure's `block_type` is **BLOCK_TYPE_BLOCKPTR_CHUNK**, and its `block_offset` points to the level 1 block chunks. While the level 2 can contain $24 * 24$ elements.

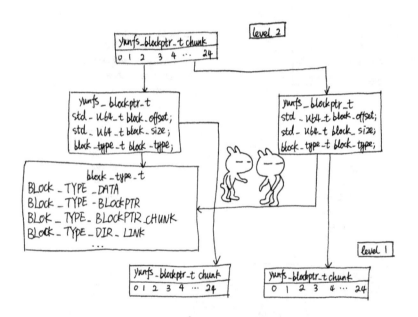

Figure 4.6   Plain file structure II

Below is the level 1 `block_ptr` chunks points to the real DATA, the `block_type` is assigned with **BLOCK_TYPE_DATA**, and `block_offset` points to the real DATA. The DATA's size is given by the `block_size` which is mentioned already and is dynamically calculated according to the file's real size.

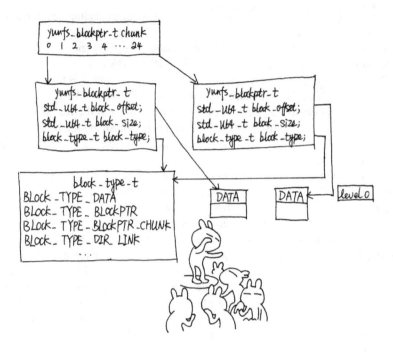

Figure 4.7   Plain file structure III

From above three pictures, you can know how to manage content for the plain file by using indirect blocks.

All above structures are the physical data stored on disk, and they are also the same structures which are cached in memory. YunFS uses caches for those operations, and will release those caches at the correct time.

4.3   The Interface Design

4.3.1   Create

Create is the major interface function of File Module, it is used to create a file or directory for the purpose of file management. There is a root directory named '/' for all those new created files or directories, and which is a common design in Unix like file system, and YunFS follows this rule. The disk object management is handled by the Disk Module, which will be introduced in the next chapter. The first thing we can know here is when we can allocate a file's disk object, which is no difference from allocating a memory object. In fact, YunFS uses memory techniques to handle the disk object management.

We can create a file or directory which shares a same interface, and with the given parameter to indicate the file's type is whether **DIRECTORY_TYPE** or **PLAIN-FILE_TYPE**. If we input the file's type as **DIRECTORY_TYPE**, it is not necessary to calculate the Directory's block size. While as **PLAINFILE_TYPE**, there will have a calculation to get the `block_size` of the plain file and the real size of the plain file should be given as input parameter. It can help improving the performance of file's reading and writing by choosing a reasonable `block_size` and also decrease of disk wastage.

If you already know basement of filesystem, you may have some ideas with the disk wastage, I would like to list some examples to emphasize the concept of disk wastage. For example, there is a file whose real size is 11M, if we assign 2M as the `block_size` of this file, then take a simple calculation, it will have enough space to store the file in 6 blocks. The disk wastage is equal to 2*6 - 11 about 1M, and the wastage rate is about 1/12. What a big waste is it! Following let us assign 1M as the file's `block_size`, the file can be entirely stored in 11 blocks and the disk wastage is ZERO! From above some extreme examples we can know that it is very important to choose a correct `block_size` of the file. The `block_size` of Google's GFS is 64M, so GFS is not designed for small files, but for large and huge files. Though GFS have some special ways to chunk small files into a large file with an internal index, its major target is focused on large and huge files.

It will have different options for creating function when uses input parameter, you can decide to choose preallocated blocks whether or not when creating a plain file. This is an important feature for modern file systems. If choosing delay allocating blocks, create function will run very fast when dealing with a chunk of new files.

As mentioned before, since YunFS is designed as a full memory operational filesystem, it has dropped the on disk B+ tree design which is usually used in traditional filesystem. The B+ tree's merge, split, balance and search are operated mainly on disk. To search a file with the full path, this searching process needs travel the B+ tree on disk, the counts of disk reading is depends on the B+ tree's nodes. YunFS does not store any B+ tree like information on disk, but stores traditional linked entry table on disk. YunFS holds a global AVL tree in memory to cache directories and files, so most searching is complete memory operation. It is an obvious advantage of full memory operation that it can speed up the performance. With the memory becoming more and more cheap, it is a good time to design YunFS as a full memory operational filesystem. Though SSD's reading is already much better than traditional magnet disk, it is still 100X slower than memory.

YunFS's disk storage is based on cloud storage, which is WAN side disk storage. To read a data, YunFS's storage will take a request to the remote cloud storage and download object file from remote to local. You can imagine how slowly to read a disk file, so on disk searching technical like B+ tree is not suitable for Cloud Storage based filesystem.

Till now, the directory entry is still using the technique of linked table, to improve it in future, YunFS will import hash directory entry, this improvement could greatly accelerate searching speed.

The COW feature is a modern file system's landmark feature, it is the abrasive of Copy On Write. What it means? In fact, the concept of COW is easy, it is to take a copy when you want to write a new one. For example, if you want to insert a new file to a directory, the system will create a new entry to hold it, the file's parent directory entry also needs to take a copy, and the whole procedure will recursive up to the Root directory. After the operation finished, the Root directory will point to the new node. The COW can make sure that the transaction is consistent from the root of the target with the new created file. The COW is also the implementation technique of the snapshot with the filesystem.

If you often use Dropbox, you may notice that the file stored in Dropbox does have a revision feature with that you can revert the file to its history file. And the revision feature is helpful if you modify a file frequently and sometime want to see the file's history. Also, this revision feature is provided by COW, when a file is modified COW will always take a copy with old nodes. It assigns a revision number to the old node as 1.0 version and the new node as 2.0 version, so it has two revision numbers of the file, this is the theory of revision implementation. The snapshot of a filesystem has the same design theory. The advantage of COW is that all the files can be revised if needed. When you take some wrong losing a file, you still have a chance to revert it, even you want to revert to a history revision, it is very easy. In the other word, this filesystem does the same work as a revision system like CVS, SVN or GIT. However, it will cost much more disk to record information with a history of too many revisions, that is COW's shortcoming. To resolve this problem, you can clean the revision history. Also to avoid too much disk space occupied by revision history, it is only 3 last revisions are permitted, all previous will be deleted automatically, this wonderful function is my target perfect file's revision feature, I will keep working to achieve it.

```
1
2  function calculate_block_size(file_size)
3  {
4      var disk_tb[] = [512, 1024, 2*1024, 4*1024, 8*1024,
           ... 8*1024*1024];
5      var score = [];
6      for(i = 0; i < disk_tb.size; i++){
7          count = ceil(file_size/disk_tb[i]);
8          total_size = count * disk_tb[i];
9          wastage = 1 - file_size/total_size;
10         score[i] = wastage*200 + count;
11
12         if (i == 0 || score[i] < min_score){
13             min_score = score[i];
14             min_index = i;
15         }
16     }
```

```
17        block_size = disk_tb[min_index];
18    }
```

Listing 4.1   calculate_block_size(file_size)

- The algorithm of calculating `block_size`
  The `block_size` table is listed as below, from the smallest 512 bytes to 8M as one `block_size`. The algorithm can choose proper `block_size` to satisfy the requirements from small files to large files.

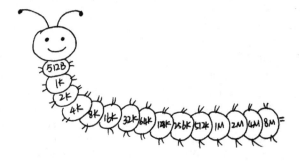

Figure 4.8   block size list

We use a score algorithm to determine the `block_size`, here below three variables should be calculated

- block counts
  The block counts are calculated by $file\_size/block\_size$

- wastage percent
  The waste percent is calculated by $1 - file\_size/(count * block\_size)$

- score
  The score is equal to $wastage * 200 + count$

We can take a loop calculation with above block size lists, and choose the lowest score as the best one of the `block_size` lists. With this score algorithm, it is able to keep balance between count number and disk wastage. As we know that the level of indirect blocks will become smaller with the small block count number. It is helpful for the smaller levels to gain better performance on the reading and writing of a plain file. So the block counts take a higher portion in the algorithm. It will waste less storage disk with a smaller wastage percent, which takes also a portion in the algorithm. All above show us the score algorithm's details with `block_size`.

```
1
2   function file_create(fullpath, type, data, data_size)
3   {
4       exist = check_file_exist(fullpath);
5       if (exist){
6           return;
7       }
8       parent_directory = parse_parent_from_fullpath(fullpath
                );
9       filename = parse_filename_from_fullpath(fullpath);
10
11
12      parent_node = find_file_node(parent_directory);
13      if (parent_node == 0){
14          return;
15      }
16
17      p_node = file_alloc_new_node( yunfs_node_phys_t);
18      switch(type){
19      case NODE_TYPE_DIRECTORY:
20          p_node->node_type = NODE_TYPE_DIRECTORY;
21          p_dir_link = file_alloc_new_node(
                yunfs_dir_link_t)
22          p_node->node_blockptr.block_type =
                BLOCK_TYPE_DIR_LINK;
23          p_node->node_blockptr.block_offset = DISK_OFFSET(
                p_dir_link);
24
25      case NODE_TYPE_PLAINFILE:
26          p_node->node_type = NODE_TYPE_PLAINFILE;
27          p_node->attr.block_size = calculate_block_size(
                size);
28          p_node->attr.size  = size;
29
30          if (options.prealloc_enabled){
31              alloc_indirect_blocks(p_node);
32          }
33      }
34      append_file_entry_to_parent_directory(parent_node,
                filename, p_node);
35      append_global_avl_tree(fullpath, DISK_OFFSET(p_node));
36  }
```

Listing 4.2 file_create(fullpath, type, data, data_size)

❹ It will at beginning check whether the file exist or not, if affirmative no need to do anything but just return.

❽ Parse the parent directory and file name from the full path

⑫ Obtain the directory's parent node, if this parent node does not exist, the parent directory would not exist yet, yet at this time nothing need to do but just return. With the directory concept in the filesystem, the parent directory is dependent by the file and it can't be ignored.

⑰ Call the object module's functions to allocate a new object node whose structure is yunfs_node_phys_t.

⑱ Will judge file_type is whether **DIRECTORY** or **PLAINFILE**.

⑲ If it is a directory, the program will call the File Object Module's function *file_alloc_new_node()* to allocate a new object node, this node type is DIR_LINK whose structure is yunfs_dir_link_t, then the program assigns the node_blockptr.block_offset as this new created dir_link's disk_offset. As mentioned before, all the file node has a disk offset which points the storage location on disk.

㉕ If it is a plain file, it will at first take a block size calculation to choose the most proper block_size, I already introduced this algorithm in the above section. If the inputting options are marked as preallocate, it will call a function to allocate all indirect blocks according to the file's real size. If we are able to preallocate indirect blocks here,would not to allocate those nodes in future.

㉞ Append the file name of the parent directory entry, once done, the parent directory does contain the new created nodes.

㉟ Append the full path and disk offset to the global AVL tree, this action plays the role as a fast path in searching improved performance.

```
1
2  function append_file_entry_to_parent_directory(parent_node,
        filename, node)
3  {
4      dir_link = disk_read_block(parent_node.node_blockptr.
           block_offset);
5      do {
6          for (i = 0; i < DIR_LINK_ENTRY;  i++){
7              if( dir_link->dir_entry[i] == 0){
```

```
8          dir_attr = disk_alloc_new_block( yunfs_dir_attr_t);
9                    dir_attr->name = filename;
10         dir_attr->block_id = DISK_OFFSET(node);
11          dir_link->dir_entry[i] = DISK_OFFSET(dir_attr);
12         }
13             }
14           dir_next = dir_link ->dir_next
15           if (dir_next == 0){
16               dir_link = disk_read_block(dir_link ->
                      dir_next);
17           }else {
18               new_dir_next = disk_alloc_new_block(
                      yunfs_dir_link_t);
19               dir_link->dir_next = DISK_OFFSET(
                      new_dir_next);
20               dir_link = new_dir_next;
21           }
22      while(1);
23  }
```

Listing 4.3   append_file_entry_to_parent_directory(parent_node, filename, node)

❹ Call the disk module to read the data from disk to get a `dir_link` structure.

❺ Take a while loop to find an available empty directory entry slot. If found, call the disk module to allocate an attribute block, then assign the file name and block offset to this attribute block node. After all, those finished, take an assignment to the `dir_link`'s empty entry to this new allocated directory attribute block.

⑱ It is going to take a link with next directory link. YunFS used a linked directory entry to hold all child files or directories. If the current directory entry is full, it will be the right time to allocate a new directory link block.

㉓ All above are the postcode codes to show the basic logic of `append_file_to_parent_entry` function.

```
1
2   function alloc_indirect_blocks(node)
3   {
4       #define  BLOCKPTR_COUNT 24
5       check_node_type_is_plain_file();
6
7       block_count = ceil(node->attr.size/node->attr.
            block_size);
8       if (block_count <  BLOCKPTR_COUNT){
9          level = 1;
10      }else if (block_count <  BLOCKPTR_COUNT^2){
```

```
11          level = 2;
12      }else if (block_count <  BLOCKPTR_COUNT^4){
13          level = 3;
14      }else if (block_count <  BLOCKPTR_COUNT^6){
15          level = 4;
16      }
17
18      if (node->node_levels < level){
19          block_chunk = disk_alloc_new_block(BLOCKPTR_COUNT
                * sizeof(stl_u64_t));
20          node-> node_blockptr.block_offset = DISK_OFFSET(
              block_chunk);
21          node->node_blockptr.block_size = BLOCKPTR_COUNT *
                sizeof(stl_u64_t);
22          node->node_blockptr.block_type =
              BLOCK_TYPE_BLOCKPTR_CHUNK;
23          node->node_levels = level;
24      }  else {
25          block_chunk = disk_block_read(DISK_OFFSET(node->
              node_blockptr.block_offset));
26      }
27
28
29
30      inline_alloc_indirect_blocks(block_chunk, node->
          node_levels);
31  }
32
33
34
35  alloc_block = 0;
36  function inline_alloc_indirect_blocks(block_chunk, level,
      max_blocks){
37          if (level == 0){
38              for (i = 0; i < BLOCKPTR_COUNT; i++){
39                  block_data = disk_alloc_new_block(
                      block_size);
40                  block_chunk[i]. block_offset =
                      DISK_OFFSET(block_data)
41                  block_chunk[i].block_size = block_size;
42                  block_chunk[i].block_type =
                      BLOCK_TYPE_DATA;
43                  alloc_block ++;
44
45                  if (alloc_block >= max_blocks){
46                      return;
47                  }
48              }
49          return;
```

```
50              }else{
51                  for (i = 0; i < BLOCKPTR_COUNT; i++){
52                      block_chunk_data = disk_alloc_new_block
                            (BLOCKPTR_COUNT * sizeof(stl_u64_t)
                            ););
53                      block_chunk[i].block_offset =
                            DISK_OFFSET(block_data)
54                      block_chunk[i].block_size =
                            BLOCKPTR_COUNT*sizeof(stl_u64_t);;
55                      block_chunk[i].block_type =
                            BLOCK_TYPE_BLOCKPTR_CHUNK;
56
57                      inline_alloc_indirect_blocks(
                            block_chunk_data, level - 1,
                            max_blocks);
58
59                      if (alloc_block >= max_blocks){
60                          return;
61                      }
62                  }
63              }
64          }
```

Listing 4.4   alloc_indirect_blocks(node)

❺ Check whether the node type is PLAIN FILE or not, only PLAIN FILE can use the function of allocating indirect block. By this way, we can validate the correct function with the correct file type.

❼ Take a calculation to obtain the level number, just like using indirect blocks to contain all the data blocks. The indirect block numbers of level are as 24^x, while 24^6 is a block as large as 191102976. If a block size is as 8M, the limitation of YunFS's largest file size is $24^6 * 8$, about 1.4T. It's fine if we don't use a huge single file at all. However YunFS can support a larger file as well if the number of level attains to 4 or even larger.

❿ It is time to create a root block chunk, which is consisted of a 24-element table, each element's size is an unsigned 64. It is a good choice to use tables in indirect block chunks. Now, I would like to describe more about how it is designed. In modern filesystem designing, there are many optimization techniques used in indirect blocks. One of the most frequently used technique is to adopt a chunk table to hold blocks. In EXT4 filesystem, it would like to allocate a large chunk table to hold those data blocks, because chunk table is used and those blocks are sequence sorted, it has a good performance in reading and writing with sequence accessing. And also this performance is closely related with hard disk's physical layout. I don't want to talk more about the hard disk's physical layout, but have more interesting in the design with a chunk table. . In YunFS, we still use the

indirect block chunk concept, which is a default feature of YunFS, so there is
no need to do something special to allocate large chunks like EXT4. In future
YunFS would like to use a dynamic indirect block chunk. Now the BLOCK
chunk count is limited to 24, in the future, this chunk count will be dynamically
calculated to have more DATA blocks kept at level 1.

36 Below is the in-line recursive callback function which handling some recursive
up. If the level is 0, we would like to allocate DATA blocks, which will be used
to store the real content data of a plain file. If level is not 0, we would allocate
a chunk table to continue the indirect block chunk table. If the allocated data
blocks get to the maximum of the data blocks, it stops recursive looping and
return back.

64 All above steps are the algorithm is implementation of how to allocate indirect
blocks. With very easy logic, all blocks must be kept under allocating until no
data left.

4.3.2 Delete

Comparing to Create, it needs to do more things for a directory's remove to recursively cleanup with the child directories. When removing a file need also to recursively cleanup with the indirect chunk blocks that holds the contents of the file. All
freed blocks will be recycled for next available usage. There is no difference between YunFS and other filesystems when deleting a file or directory. Because of
adopting the organized directory concept, it is a hard and dirty work to recursively
clean up the child directories. Till now, you may understand better why more and
more filesystems abandon the organized directory concept in their filesystem design.
Though directory can keep the files organized and clean, you had to face the phe-
nomenon that the filesystem needs to do more work to recursively clean up the child
files or child directories if removes any files. Due to it, the organized directory means
dependence, you can't directly create a file without been given a parent directory. If
its parent directory does not exist, the file system had to create one.

The AWS's S3 is the distributed object filesystem, it is very easy to create or
remove a file. The parent directory of a file has been just a character '/', no need to
take a recursive cleanup when is created or removed. Unlike to AWS's S3, YunFS
adopts the traditional filesystem's directory, so need undertake the pains in deleting.

```
1
2   function yunfs_remove(fullpath)
3   {
4       node = find_file_node(fullpath)
5       if (node == NULL){
6           return;
7       }
8
9       inline_free_directory(node);
10
```

```
11        fullpath_avl_del(fullpath);
12  }
```

Listing 4.5 yunfs_remove(fullpath)

❹ To remove a file or directory, it will firstly get the node of a file or directory, then check this node exist or not.

❾ Call the inline recursive function to free the directory's node.

⓫ Call to remove the full path from the global AVL tree, this is a fast search engine.

```
1
2   function inline_free_directory(node)
3   {
4
5       if (node->node_type == NODE_TYPE_DIRECTORY){
6           if (node->node_blockptr.block_type ==
                BLOCK_NODE_TYPE_DIR_LINK){
7               dir_link = DISK_READ(node->node_blockptr.
                    block_offset);
8               do {
9                   for (i = 0; i < DIR_LINK_ENTRY; i++){
10                      if (dir_link->dir_entry[i] == 0){
11                          continue;
12                      }
13                      child_dir_attr = DISK_READ(
                            dir_link->dir_entry[i]);
14                      child_node = DISK_READ(
                            child_dir_attr->block_id);
15
16                      inline_free_directory(child_node);
17
18
19                      DISK_FREE(child_node);
20                      DISK_FREE(child_dir_attr);
21                  }
22                  dir_link = DISK_READ(dir_link->dir_next
                        );
23              }while(1);
24          }
25      }else if (node->node_type == NODE_TYPE_PLAINFILE){
26          block_chunk = DISK_READ(node->node_blockptr.
                block_offset);
27          inline_free_indirect_blocks(block_chunk);
28          DISK_FREE(block_chunk);
29      }
```

30   }

Listing 4.6   inline_free_directory(node)

❷ The *inline_free_direcotry()* is used to remove directory recursively.

❺ It will check the node_type is DIRECTORY or PLAINFILE. If this node is DIRECTORY, it will at first get the dir_link object by reading this node's block_offset. By getting the dir_link object, it is time to walk through the dir_link's entries. As already mentioned the dir_link object is a linked table, the dir_next would point to the next table, till its end. If the dir_entry is null, the function need do nothing, while if the dir_entry is not null, it gets the child_dir_attr object and the child_node object by reading the dir_attr's block_id, Then it calls the function *inline_free_directory()* to recursively free this child node. After all is done, then take a DISK_FREE to release those two nodes. If the dir_link's dir_next points to next dir_link, it needs to get the next dir_link and repeat above steps. This is the logic to recursively remove the directory.

㉕ If the node's type is PLAINFILE, it will take a loop to clean up the indirect blocks, then free this block_chunk object.

```
1
2   function inline_free_indirect_blocks(block_chunk, level)
3   {
4       if (level == 0){
5           for(i = 0; i < BLOCKPTR_COUNT; i++){
6               if(block_chunk[i].block_type ==
                    BLOCK_TYPE_DATA){
7                   DISK_FREE(block_chunk[i].block_offset);
8               }
9           }
10          return;
11      }else {
12          for (i = 0; i < BLOCKPTR_COUNT; i++){
13              if(block_chunk[i].block_type ==
                    BLOCK_TYPE_BLOCKPTR_CHUNK){
14                  child_block_chunk = DISK_READ(
                        block_chunk[i].block_offset);
15                  inline_free_indirect_blocks(
                        child_block_chunk, level-1);
16                  DISK_FREE(child_block_chunk);
17              }
18          }
19      }
20  }
```

Listing 4.7   inline_free_indirect_blocks(block_chunk, level)

❹ If level is 0, it means that all the nodes are DATA blocks, in this situation, this procedure can call the
DISK_FREE() function to free those DATA blocks. We use indirect objects to hold all the content of a file, when the level of indirect blocks is 0, the object will point to a DATA block, which stores the real data of a file.

⑪ If level is not 0, the codes in above drawing will take a loop with
BLOCKPTR_COUNT and verify whether the element of block_chunk is CHUNK type, the codes will read the child block_chunk and call the *inline_free_indirect_blocks()* to take a recursive loop to free all the indirect block chunks. In the end, the codes will call *DISK_FREE()* to free this chunk object.

⑮ We use the recursive call function to free those indirect blocks, in this condition the logic is clear. It is known that the recursive dirty cleanup work needs to be done with a directorial concept, However a distributed object filesystem with a key-value concept, does not need to do this recursive work. Something gained also means something lost!

4.3.3 GetAttr

This function is used to get the file's attributes including permit, create time, size and owner etc. The internal implementation of *yunfs_getattr()* is simple, all file attributes can be obtained by reading the attribute block of the file.

```
1
2  function yunfs_getattr(fullpath, attr)
3  {
4
5      node = find_file_node(fullpath)
6      if (node == NULL){
7          return;
8      }
9      attr->file_type = node->node_type;
10     attr->size = node->attr.size;
11     attr->birth = node->attr.birth;
12     attr->owner = node->attr.owner;
13     attr->permit = node->attr.permit;
14 }
```

Listing 4.8   yunfs_getattr(fullpath, attr)

❷ The function *yunfs_getattr()* is used to get the attributes of a file, including size, birth, owner, and permit.

❺ The internal function is simple to get the node of the file. If the node exists, return to its attribute to the end-user.

4.3.4 Read and Write

The *yunfs_read()* and *yunfs_write()* function is the only way to read or write the content of a file. The read/write procedure will take a travel in file's indirect blocks and read the DATA block which is marked as level 0. Given the offset and read/write size, the function can read/write the data from any offset of the file with a fixed size. The following drawing shows the layout of indirect blocks which holds the content of the file. The `block_type` is **BLOCK_TYPE_DATA** and the offset points to the location of DATA.

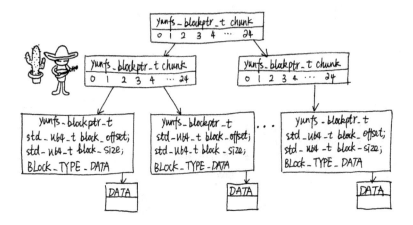

Figure 4.9   read or write structure

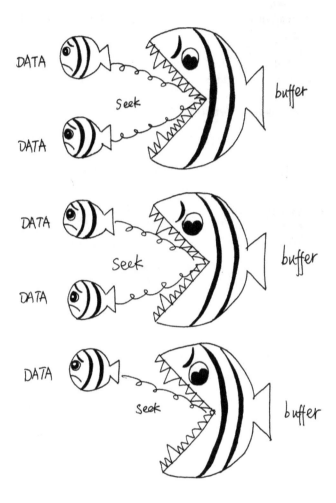

Figure 4.10   buffer eats the data

- This is the sample plain file which has 4 full DATA and a partial DATA, will keep being filled with buffer to load the data repeatedly until all the content of the file read completely.

- If the seek is 0, the full DATA1 and DATA2 will fulfill the buffer, then the first read finish and return fulfilled buffer to the client.

- At the second reading, the full DATA3 and DATA4 will fulfill the buffer, then return fulfilled buffer to the client.

- At the third read, it will load the remaining DATA5 to buffer. The plain file's content is read completely.

- Three times reading, the seek will point to the end of the file, due to it, it cannot continue the reading anymore.

4.3.4.1   Inline_read_write_indirect

```
1
2   function inline_read_write_indirect(block_chunk, level,
        seek, buf, buf_size)
3   {
4       if (level == 0){
5
6           for(i = 0; i < BLOCKPTR_COUNT; i++){
7               if(block_chunk[i].block_type ==
                    BLOCK_TYPE_DATA){
8                   read_count = read_size/
                        data_size_per_block;
9
10                  if (seek){
11                      if (real_readwrite_size >=
                            buf_size){
12                          return;
13                      }
14                      if (seek /data_size_per_block ==
                            read_count){
15                          DATA= DISK_READ(block_chunk[i
                                ].block_offset);
16                          offset = seek%
                                data_size_per_block;
17                          size = buf_size:
                                data_size_per_block -
                                seek%data_size_per_block;
18                          buffer = DATA[offset:size];
19                      }else if ((seek + buf_size)/
                            data_size_block == read_count)
                            {
20                          DATA= DISK_READ(block_chunk[i
                                ].block_offset);
21                          offset = 0;
22                          size = (seek + buf_size)%
                                data_size_block;
23                          buffer = DATA[offset:size];
24                      }else if (real_readwrite_size){
25                          DATA= DISK_READ(block_chunk[i
                                ].block_offset);
26                          offset = real_readwrite_size;
```

```
27                          size =data_size_block;
28                          buffer = DATA[offset:size];
29                      }else {
30                          read_size = read_size +
                                data_size_per_block;
31                      }
32                  }
33
34
35              else{
36
37                  if (data_size /data_size_per_block
                        == read_count &&
38                      data_size % data_size_per_block
                            ){
39                      DATA= DISK_READ(block_chunk[i
                            ].block_offset);
40                      offset = read_count *
                            data_size_per_block;
41                      size = data_size%
                            data_size_per_block;
42                      buffer = DATA[offset:size];
43                  }else {
44
45                      DATA= DISK_READ(block_chunk[i
                            ].block_offset);
46                      offset = seek%
                            data_size_per_block;
47                      size = buf_size:
                            data_size_per_block -
                            seek%data_size_per_block;
48                      buffer = DATA[offset:size];
49
50                  }
51
52              }
53          }
54      }
55
56
57  }else {
58      for (i = 0; i < BLOCKPTR_COUNT; i++){
59          if(block_chunk[i].block_type ==
                BLOCK_TYPE_BLOCKPTR_CHUNK){
60              child_block_chunk = DISK_READ(
                    block_chunk[i].block_offset);
61              inline_read_write_indirect(
                    child_block_chunk, level-1, seek,
                    buf, buf_size);
```

```
62                    }
63                }
64           }
65  }
```

Listing 4.9   inline_read_write_indirect(block_chunk, level, seek, buf, buf_size)

❷ It is the recursive callback function to read or write data.

❹ If the level is 0, it means the block points to the DATA, at this level, the program can realize its target to read or write the real content of the file.

❽ Check the seek is 0 or not, the result will bring different behavior.

㉚ During the first reading, when the seek is 0, we can respect the logic described as follows: If the DATA size is larger than the buffer, we can read the partial DATA into buffer. However, if the DATA size is smaller than the buffer, we can read the full DATA into buffer.

Continue to fill the next DATA to the buffer until the buffer is completely filled. If the current block chunk looped completely, we continue to call the recursive callback function to take a loop with the next block chunk.

❷ At the second read when the seek is not 0, we will take a travel in the location of the seeking. The read_count saves the counts of how many DATA nodes have been travelled.

If the DATA of the current seek is located, the DATA's content from offset to the end of DATA will be loaded, and all data will be copied to the buffer or be written to the disk.

Continue the loop with the DATA and copy next data to the buffer until the buffer is completely filled.

After all DATA are travelling, it will copy the rest size of the DATA of the buffer, it is necessary to avoid overwriting or overriding.

If read till the end of the plain file, it will copy the remaining files to the buffer or disk. .

㊽ Traveling the block_chunk table to call this inline recursive callback function *inline_read_write_indirect* and keep repeating the same logic of the above codes.

4.3.4.2   Read&write

```
1
2  function yunfs_read_write(fullpath, seek, buf, buf_size)
3  {
4
```

```
5        node = find_file_node(fullpath)
6        if (node == NULL || node->node_type !=
             NODE_TYPE_PLAINFILE){
7            return;
8        }
9
10       block_chunk = DISK_READ(node->node_blockptr.
             block_offset);
11       inline_read_write_indirect(block_chunk, node->
             node_levels - 1, seek, buf, buf_size);
12   }
```

Listing 4.10   yunfs_read_write(fullpath, seek, buf, buf_size)

❺ At first the function will search to get the node of the file, if the file does not exist or the file is not a plain file, it will return. It is only a plain file which can be read by this function to get the content of the file.

❻ If file's size is zero, the function could read nothing and have to return.

❿ Read the disk to get the block chunk object.

⓫ Call the recursive callback file to read the content and fill the content to the buffer. This function is used to read or write data from or to disk, because reading is similar as writing. The target of both reading and writing is buffer or disk.

4.3.5 ReadDir

The Linux's `ls` command will display all the file lists of the current directory. The internal implementation of `ls` is processed by *yunfs_readdir()* function which will return the current directory file lists one by one when the client recursively calling it. The implementation and function's definition in YunFS is same as Linux.

After the travel with the last file under a directory, the *yunfs_readdir()* will return NULL, it means that this is the last file in the directory, and will halt the while looping.

The *yunfs_readdir()* is always called together with *yunfs_getattr()*, after getting the node block of a file, then use *yunfs_getattr()* to get file's attribute information which consists of the file's name, type, size and create time etc.

```
1
2    function yunfs_readdir(fullpath, dirent)
3    {
4
5        node = find_file_node(fullpath)
6        if (node == NULL){
7            return;
```

```
8          }
9      if (dirent->name == 0){
10         isnext = true;
11     }
12
13     if (node->node_type == NODE_TYPE_DIRECTORY){
14         if (node->node_blockptr.block_type ==
               BLOCK_NODE_TYPE_DIR_LINK){
15             dir_link = DISK_READ(node->node_blockptr.
                   block_offset);
16             do {
17                 for (i = 0; i < DIR_LINK_ENTRY; i++){
18                     if (dir_link->dir_entry[i] == 0){
19                         continue;
20                     }
21                     child_dir_attr = DISK_READ(
                           dir_link->dir_entry[i]);
22                     child_node = DISK_READ(
                           child_dir_attr->block_id);
23
24                     if (isnext == true){
25                         dirent->file_type =
                               child_node->node_type;
26                         dirent->name = child_dir_attr
                               ->name;
27                         return;
28                     }
29                     if (child_dir_attr->name == dirent
                           ->name){
30                         isnext= true;
31                     }
32                 }
33
34
35                 dir_link = DISK_READ(dir_link->dir_next
                       );
36                 if (dir_link  == 0){
37                     if (isnext == true){
38                         dirent->file_type = 0;
39                         dirent->name = "";
40                         break;
41                     }
42                 }
43             }while(1);
44         }
45     }else if (node->node_type == NODE_TYPE_PLAINFILE){
46         dirent->file_type = 0;
47     dirent->name = "";
48     }
```

49   }

Listing 4.11   yunfs_readdir(fullpath, dirent)

❺ Get the node object with the full path of directory, if the node does not exist, do nothing but return.

❾ If the directory's name is input as NULL, the program will set the conditional variable `isnext` as true. If we are familiar with the Linux's *yunfs_readir()* function, we know that the *yunfs_readir()* is step by step return the next file within the same directory, for example the directory home' does have two files that are `file_one`, and `file_two`. When you first call the reader, the `dirent`'s name is NULL, it will return `file_one` at your first calling, and then the call will return `file_two`, and call the third time, it will return NULL. This is the common behavior of *yunfs_readir()*.

⓭ Check whether current full path's node type is a DIRECTORY, only when the node's type is DIRECTORY this function can obtain the file lists, otherwise the function will return with nothing.

⓯ If the current node's type is DIRECTORY, it will take a loop checking with its child nodes. If `isnext` is true, it means that the program finds the correct nodes, and save both file's name and type to `dirent`.

㉙ If the `dirent`'s name is equal to this node's name, we find the current node at this time, we should return its next file to end user, and set the `isnext` conditional variable as true. The function will return with the next file's attribute to end user.

㊲ The `dir_link` is a linked table, so we need to take a loop running with its' `dir_next`. If `dir_next` is zero, we reach the end of the file lists and have to return.

CHAPTER 5

THE DISK MODULE DESIGN

5.1 The Brief Description of the Disk Management

It is noted in the first chapter that the YunFS is a complete memory distributed filesystem. The disk management adopts the technique which is also used in memory management. Regarded the disk blocks as memory blocks. The block's unique address is from 0 to 2^{64}. When you allocate a disk block, the offset that represents the location of the disk block will be returned.

There is no disk volume concept in YunFS, the disk volume is abandoned because the volume's size is limited to the storage capacity. For example, you can't store a 1T file to a disk volume which only has 1G.

We combine all physical disk volumes into a very large virtual disk whose size is 2^{64} byte, and we do not care where the real data are stored in.

The table contents:

1 G	1024 M
1 M	1024 k
1 k	1024 Byte
1 Byte	8 Bit

$$1M/4k = 1024/4 = 256$$

$$1B = 8 Bit$$

$$32B = 256 Bit$$

$$1M = 32B$$

$$1G = 1024 * 32B = 32k$$

$$256 * 16 = 4k$$

Figure 5.1 handy calculate the disk costage

The bitmap is the way presenting the block's usage status, whether is already allocated or available to be used in a traditional filesystem, it uses each bit to indicate the block's status. We can easily take a calculation to represent the bitmap's disk cost with an example that the disk size is 1G and the block size is 4k. The 1M disk has 256 blocks, $256/8 = 32$ bytes. To indicate a 1M disk, we need a bitmap which has 32 bytes, $1G = 32 * 1024 = 32k$. While to indicate a 1G disk, we need a bitmap which has 32k. If we don't use the bitmap, but use a space-map to represent the block's usage status, the disk's cost is less. In YunFS, we used an 8M-size slab to represent the 1M disk, $1024/8 = 256$, we use 256 slabs, each slab has a metadata to represent the usage status information, and the size of metadata is 16 bytes, so $256 * 16 = 4k$, the size of space-map is $256 * 0$, it is no need to use spacemap but to set a flag with free in attribute, it means that the slab is free and available to use. The total size of using slab is 4K, it is 8x less than bitmap's 32k. Less disk cost helps us pay less money for a cloud storage as we know that bigger disk costs more money and save disk space means saving money.

The disk management adopts the slab memory technique to manage the disk blocks. The slab technique is greatly useful to manage the small files, as well as the large files. The space-map lists are encoded and stored on the physical disk. When loading space-map lists from disk into memory, the space-map lists will be decoded to a space-map table. If the slab is free, it is no need to store any space-map lists, just set a free flag to the slab, it means that the slab is free and available. If the slab is full, it does not need to use space-map lists neither, this is the advantage of using a space-map to represent with disk block's status usage. Because we use a range to describe the usage status of disk blocks. More and more modern filesystems are designed to use the range instead of bitmap to represent the usage status of disk blocks, such as ZFS. YunFS has propriety in its design of the disk management, uses slab memory management to manage the disk blocks, and lock-free is its important feature in block allocations. The YunFS's disk management used also cache and slab to manage the disk blocks. There is a cache table that represents the a serial of fixed block space which can be allocated by user, please see Figure 5.3 Cache Table.

The slab's metadata is stored on the disk, and it will be loaded into memory on demand. Normally it will not need to be loaded into the memory cache if it is in FULL status. But cache the slab when is taken off some free of objects, and the slab will be added into the cache's partial list.

The cache has a high cache which is thread independence. The allocation of disk objects in multiple threads can be 'lock free'.

The disk management adopts the design of memory buffered IO, so IO operations are queued into IO queue, when dealing with the dirty disk blocks. The buffered IO will be scheduled at another time to take a synchronization to disk with a task queue, and there is no blocking operation when the IO is writing to the slow disk.

The dirty IO queue is the queue which is used to take a synchronization later with the disk, it will be cleared after finishing the synchronization. And the clean IO queue is the queue for those read only IO buffer. If an IO buffer is used for reading an object, this IO buffer will not be queued to the dirty IO queue but to the clean IO queue. If no more use longer this IO buffer will be released to save memory. Keep the IO buffer fresh and sync frequently without blocking is the logic which is very simple.

The checksum uses a Hash64 algorithm to take a checksum calculation and validation with the IO buffer, if the checksum does not change, and the IO buffer is clean, we do not need to take physical synchronize with the disk, even it is in dirty queue, it is the basic logic of synchronicity in dirty IO queue.

When I begin to design YunFS' disk management, I use another simple way to record the usage status of disk blocks, and do not take the slab management into consideration. But later, after experiencing with the development of YunFS, I find that the disk management is more like a big memory pool management, I can use the pool to allocate or free the blocks and to read or write with the IO buffer to speed up the handling process without blocking. With the exploration of encoding and decoding of the space-map lists to the object-map table, this slab memory technique is proven to be suitable for the disk block management, and also proven to be able to save the disk space comparing to the bitmap. The slab block management is very good for small memory blocks without fragment, it is helpful in the management with small files. This is the nature feature of YunFS by design, we avoid using another technique like ext4, which uses a large chunk block file to hold on many small files to avoid the small fragments and to improve the performance, this ext4's chunk technique is not a naturalistic design but a patch design.

In future, the disk management will much better in decreasing disk wastage by compressing the slab meta structure and `space-map` lists.

5.2   The Design and Implementation of the Disk Management Module

5.2.1   The Disk Layout Design

The physical layout of the disk is described in below drawing, the **DEV_SPEC** is like a `super-block` to describe the device information, and following is the HIGH CACHE table, the high cache entry is used to store the available disk objects which can be used later, like a fast picking table.

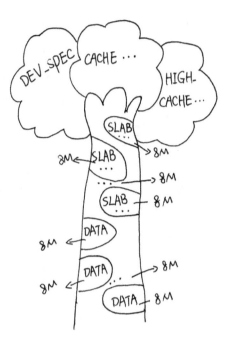

Figure 5.2   device spec layout structure

The **DEV_SPEC** is the key structure which holds on some magic information to verify whether the YunFS disk is valid or not. This **DEV_SPEC** is more like a `super-block` as traditional filesystem usually uses. The cache table is listed from the smallest object size as 128Byte to the largest object size as 8M, the objects are divided into those fixed sizes by slab management.

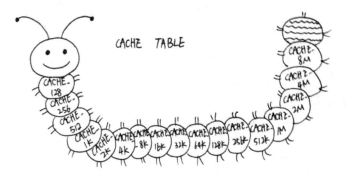

Figure 5.3 Cache table

The SLAB physical structure is stored next to the high cache, it is the meta structure to manage the DATA, and the size of DATA is about 8M. We use the slab which is located out of the disk block. Due to it, with the sequence stored slabs we can easily load more slab meta structures in memory with less IO operations. An 8M DATA can hold about $8 * 1024 * 1024/16$ about 512K counts of slab structures, and an 8M slab structure can manage a 4T size disk. In the future, we shall take a compression with the slab-meta structures, to make a less slab meta structure to manage more large disk. Obviously, the slab needs not to be loaded into memory, if the slab is fully used.

The slab will be required to load into memory when its corresponding disk is used. And this slab can be used in memory, later to allocate or free some disk's objects. Most time the slab does not need to be loaded into memory if there is no corresponding disk object allocation or release.

The DATA area is located next to a chunk of SLABs, it is the area to store real data. An 8G slab meta can manage a 8P disk, so it will leave enough slab disk space. Although the YunFS can manage a disk as large as 2^{64}, in real usage, we always cannot fully use such a large disk, the disk space is totally enough.

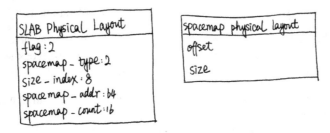

Figure 5.4   space_map structure

Both slab physical disk layout and the space-map physical layout are described in the above drawing. You may notice that the above disk layout does not leave the area to the `space-map` physical. Ho, ho, The `space-map` physical objects requested by allocation are stored in DATA area, and it can be freed with the similar logic. There is no difference from the `space-map` object to other objects. As mentioned before, if the SLAB is in FREE or FULL status, they would not need `space-map` object lists, that is the reason why we can use with smaller meta-disk than that bitmap used.

5.2.2 The Interface Design

5.2.2.1 disk_alloc_block()

```
1
2    function disk_alloc_block(size)
3    {
4        cache = avl_cache_get(size);
5        high_cache = cache->high_cache;
6        if ( high_cache->avail >= 0){
7            ptr = high_cache->cache[high_cache->avail];
8            high_cache->cache[high_cache->avail--] = 0;
9        }else {
10           ptr = cache_refill(cache, high_cache);
11       }
12       return ptr;
13   }
```

Listing 5.1   disk_alloc_block(size)

❷ *disk_alloc_block( )* is the function which is used to allocate disk block to the user, the input parameter size is also the block size which user wants to be allocated. In traditional filesystem the block size is fixed, people usually don't have the concept to allocate different block size for usage, but YunFS provides different block sizes, so the user needs pass block size as input parameter.

❹ Get the cache from the size, as mentioned before, the cache table lists all the fixed block sizes which can be allocated from the smallest block size 128Byte to 8M. With the size as the input parameter, we can obtain the cache object.

❺ Get the high cache from the cache object, high cache is useful in high pressure allocation, we can directly pick an available object to use without extra other operations. When we want to allocate chunks of the fixed disk blocks, the high cache will show off its power.

❿ If the high cache is empty, we need to take a refill with the high cache. This operation maybe spend some CPU time by having the high cache to be refilled, besides allocating a new slab if necessary.

```
1
2   function cache_refill(cache, high_cache)
3   {
4       high_cache->avail++;
5
6   redo:
7       if (!list_empty(cache->part_list_head){
8           slab = list_pull(cache->part_list_head);
9       }else if (!list_empty(cache->free_list_head){
10          slab = list_pull(cache->free_list_head);
11      }else {
12          slab = alloc_new_slab();
13      }
14
15
16      fill_high_cache(cache, slab);
17
18
19      if (slab->free == OBJ_MAP_END){
20              slab->flag = SLAB_FLAG_FULL;
21              list_add(cache->full_list_head);
22          }else if (slab->flag == SLAB_FLAG_FREE) {
23              slab->flag = SLAB_FLAG_PART;
24              list_add(cache->part_list_head);
25      }
26      if (high_cache ->avail <= MAX_CACHE_LIMIT - 16){
27          goto redo;
28      }
29
```

```
30        obj = high_cache->cache[high_cache->avail];
31        high_cache->cache[high_cache->avail --] = 0;
32        return obj;
33  }
```

Listing 5.2   cache_refill(cache, high_cache)

❷ *cache_refill()* is used to have the high cache filled with the disk objects.

❼ It will get a slab from its partial list when the parts list is empty, otherwise check the free list. If all above two partial and free lists are empty, we had to allocate a new slab for usage. With a new slab, the disk usage will expand. For example, the current disk usage is about 8G, if we allocate a new slab, the new disk usage will become $8G + 8M$.

❿ Then program keeps filling the high cache with the slab's free objects until the high cache is fully filled. If not, repeat above steps. During those steps, we check the slab's status, and put the slab into correct list, which is full list or partial list.

㉚ Since the high cache is fully filled, then we can simply choose the last available object and return this object back.

㉝ All above codes is the disk slab management behavior, with high caches, we can allocate chunks of disk objects without special add-on works. And the high cache will always keep being filled, so in most time, the speed of the disk object allocation is very fast.

5.2.2.2 disk_free_block(offset)

```
1
2   function disk_free_block(offset)
3   {
4        slab_offset = SLAB_OFFSET(offset);
5        slab = avl_slab_find(slab_offset);
6        cache = slab->cache;
7        high_cache = cache->high_cache;
8
9        if (high_cache->avail < MAX_CACHE_LIMIT -1){
10            high_cache->cache[++high_cache->avail] = offset;
11       }else {
12            cache_shirk(cache);
13       }
14  }
```

Listing 5.3   disk_free_block(offset)

❷ *disk_free_block()* function is used to free the unused disk object, if we want to delete a file or a directory, we can call this free block function to release the disk blocks.

❹ Get the slab offset from the object offset. Because the slab meta data is arranged in sequence, after taking some calculation we can obtain the slab's offset.

❺ With the slab's offset, we can obtain the slab object, this is required on demand. If the slab is not loaded into memory, the program has to load this slab into memory from disk.

❻ Get the cache object from the slab's cache index, as well as the high cache object.

❿ In most of time, if the high cache is available to be inserted, simply insert this just freed block offset into the high cache table and return. It is important to keep object reusable.

⓬ If the high cache table is fulfilled, we need to take the high cache shirk, it means that we have too many free disk objects to use and we need to take a shirk cleanup with the high cache table.

```
1
2  function disk_cache_shirk(cache, high_cache)
3  {
4      for (; high_cache->avail > MAX_CACHE_LIMIT - 16;
           high_cache->avail --){
5          offset = high_cache->cache[high_cache->avail];
6
7          slab_offset = SLAB_OFFSET(offset);
8          slab = avl_slab_find(slab_offset);
9
10
11         SET_OBJ_MAP_FREE(slab, offset);
12
13
14         if (slab->active_objects == 0){
15             slab->flag = SLAB_FLAG_FREE;
16             list_add(cache->free_list_head);
17         }else if (slab->flag == SLAB_FLAG_FULL) {
18             slab->flag = SLAB_FLAG_PART;
19             list_add(cache->part_list_head);
20         }
21     }
22 }
```

❷ *disk_cache_shirk()* is used to take the shirk with the high cache table, because there are too many available disk objects in the high cache table.

❹ Get the object's offset from the high cache's `avail`, after taking some calculation with the object's offset we can obtain the slab's offset, then get the slab object from slab's offset, this is the similar logic as above function

❿ Mark the slab's object-map with free status according to the offset.

⓮ According to the slab's newest status, put it into the corresponding list which is a free list or a partial list.

㉒ All above codes are the logic of freeing disk objects. Similar as allocation, in most time, to free a disk object is a simple put and then return.

5.2.2.3 disk_init()

If not been initialized before the disk will take an initialization to build up the layout of the disk and to leave space to the device DEV SPEC structure, cache area, high cache area and slab area. If the disk initialization is finished, next time the YunFS can directly load corresponding data structures into the memory.

5.2.2.4 space-map to obj-map decoding and encoding

The space-map list is used to take management with the disk objects. It will be synchronized to the disk in `space-map` lists, and be loaded into memory as `obj-map`. Following drawing tell us how the `space-map` takes encoding to `obj-map`, and how the `obj-map` decodes back into `space-map` list

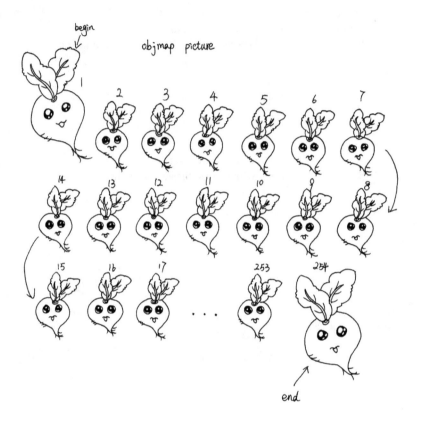

Figure 5.5   obj_map link from 0 to 254

This is the objmap table which is consisted of 254 elements. The beginning of the table is 0, and the end of the table is 254. The 0 points to 1, 1 points to 2, ... 253 points 254 and 254 points 0.

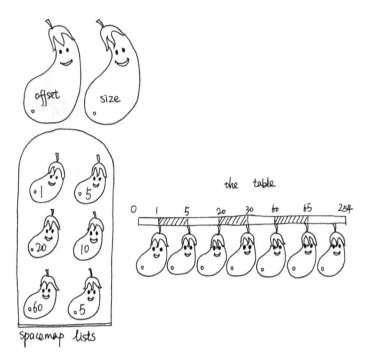

Figure 5.6   space_map structure

This is a space-map lists example, it has with three space-maps to represent the disk usage. The first space-map's offset is 1 and its size is 5. The second space-map's offset is 20 and its size is 10. The third space-map's offset is 30 and its size 5. We can present the usage of whole obj-map's table with just three space-map elements.

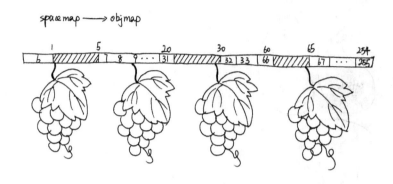

Figure 5.7   obj_map encoded to or back from space_map

This is the drawing which shows off the converting from the space-map lists to objmap table. The first space-map's offset is 1 and its size is 5, it means that the objmap table's element 1,2,3,4,5 is marked as USE.

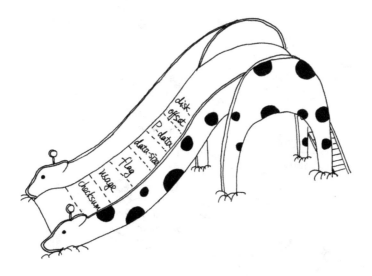

Figure 5.8   io_buffer structure

5.2.2.5 IO Buffer

The IO buffer structure will be created automatically together with the allocation of the disk object. All the writing of disk object will be complete at first in the buffer, later the modified IO buffer in memory will be synchronized to disk. If the disk object is freed, the corresponding IO buffer will also be freed at the same time.

5.2.3   The Sync Task Design

5.2.3.1 sync_worker

The sync worker will do the dirty works of the disk management. Its mission is to synchronize the dirty IO buffers to disk in order to keep the data consistent between memory and disk. Another important mission is to take synchronization with the in memory slab's meta information and its `space-map` list to disk.

Figure 5.9   Sync are working

* Take a travel in the dirty queue, then finish the dirty job of each node. The dirty job is to synchronize modified IO buffers to the slow disk. When the dirty job is finished, this dirty queue will be cleared. This dirty queue is used for the normal disk objects.

* The `space-map` lists take encoding from object maps of slab, then take sync with those dirty `space-map` lists.

* Take dirty queue with the special slab nodes.

* Take dirty queue with High Cache lists.

* The IO buffer is cleaned up, we already know the memory's recycle management, the technique is similar to the one that takes clean with the unused memory.

CHAPTER 6

THE CLOUD STORAGE MODULE DESIGN

6.1   The Brief Description of LRU Cloud Storage Module

With the popularity of cloud computing, it is the time of cloud storage. We store more frequently files to the cloud storage than to local disk. What's the reason? We use more mobile devices like the iPhone and the iPad than before. It is easy to Keep files synchronized in those mobile devices if we store files in the cloud. It is not a time to copy by hands files in devices of USB disk. And with the price of the cloud storage becomes lower than before, we are also more familiar with those cloud storage, it is also important that the cloud storage are announced to be with a 100% stability. However, the local disk may damage by some unpredictable reasons like a sudden power missing or a shock.

The cloud storage has multiple backup techniques to protect the storage, so they announce the 100% stability is not a joke, it is true indeed. YunFS is based on the cloud storage which is regarded as its disk storage, it is benefiting from those cloud storage's 100% stability.

Figure 6.1   welcome cloud storage module

As the Bitcoin is popular in the world, we know that the Bitcoin's block chain is a good choice to store a large file which will be divided into many pieces, and append a hash value to each piece to make sure the piece is correct without damage. And with the help of those pieces, we are not forced to download the complete file again, even a certain piece is possibly damaged. It is an important design with pieces to save the network traffic and the transfer time so that YunFS adopts the same technique to divide the large file into pieces. How large is this file? It is about 2^{64} byte. After dividing the large file into many small pieces, the size of one piece is 8M. It is a trade off to choose 8M as one piece's size between the network traffic and transfer time. If the size is too large, it will spend more transfer time and cause more traffic in the network. If too small it needs to download more pieces, so it is necessary to take a trade off to choose the piece's size. We have already experienced much more from the development of real project that the trade off is an important policy in system design with every decision. There is no perfect design in the world, we should take a trade off with the reality.

Figure 6.2   The disk0.bin is the first 8M disk piece of liner disk storage, from 0 to.....

YunFS chooses the cloud storage as its disk storage and also adopts the block chain. It should be noticed that the LRU cache buffer is an important feature of YunFS. We know that there is a transfer time between local disk and remote cloud storage. If we keep storing more data from remote cloud storage to local disk, the local disk has the size limitation, we can't hold all data to a same local disk. So at that time the LRU works, we only store necessary pieces of files on local disk, and the missing pieces of file will be requested on demand from the remote cloud storage. The unnecessary pieces of files will be cleaned by LRU which is the abbreviation of last recently used. The longest unused pieces of the file will be cleaned. If we want to make a layer with the data, the first layer is memory, the most frequently used data will be refreshed in memory. The second layer is local disk, the normally used data will be stored in local disk. The third layer is the remote cloud storage, we hold all the data in cloud storage, and it is requested on demand.

Each file's piece has a version number and a hash value, the version number is used to verify that the piece is synchronized correctly in distributed data consistency, we mentioned that YunFS is a distributed system, there are many YunFS instances running on the network, the piece may be modified by another YunFS instance, so it is necessary to keep the piece fresh. The hash value is used to verify the correction of piece file. If we meet some issues in piece's network transfer, we can verify the content is correct or not by the hash value.

YunFS adapts a one-leader-many-followers model in distributed system design. One leader means there is only one YunFS instance which owns the writing privilege, all other followers only own the reading privilege. If the leader modifies some pieces of a file, all other followers will get a notification about it by RAFT distributed protocol. The details of RAFT will be introduced in the next chapter.

All version and hash value of the pieces are stored in local disk, every instance of YunFS has one copy of those value tables, and those values are automatically synchronized by the RAFT distributed protocol.

We chose Amazon's S3 as YunFS's cloud storage, even we can choose another cloud storage such as Google's cloud storage. There is no difference in logic among those cloud storage provided by different companies, because they are all belong to object cloud storage. If using another cloud storage, it is simple to add a new implementation instance to YunFS 's cloud storage module. And install this new instance into YunFS, after it, switching will be activated. It is a simple way to access the remote cloud storage by using the RESTful API which is provided by the cloud storage company.

6.2   The Internal Implementation Of Cloud Storage Module

6.2.1   disk read

```
1
2  function LRU_S3_read(offset, buf, size)
3  {
4       var index = offset/FILE_SIZE;
5       var file_offset = (offset - index*FILE_SIZE)%FILE_SIZE
         ;
6       var cache = LRU_get_cache(index);
7       fseek(cache->fp, file_offset, SEEK_SET);
8       count = fread(but, 1, size, cache->fp);
9       return count;
10 }
```

Listing 6.1   LRU_S3_read(offset, buf, size)

❷ *LRU_S3_read()* is used to read the content of the file downloaded from remote cloud storage.

❹ Getting the index of the remote cloud storage file, YunFS divided the large file into 8M-size pieces which are stored in remote cloud storage. The index is the key to find the file. For example, the index with 100 means the offset of 800M.

❺ The file_offset is the offset within the file. For example 802M, its file_offset is 2M.

❻ With the index, we got the cache from the *LRU_get_cache()* function. After getting the cache structure, we read the file with the file_offset and size by using common seek and read function, finally load the data to buffer which will be returned to the user.

```
1
2  function LRU_get_cache(index)
3  {
```

```
4        var exist = raft_get_rev_hash(index, rev, hash)
5        var cache = hash_find(index);
6
7
8        if (cache != NULL){
9            if (rev == cache.rev && hash == cache.hash){
10               LRU_queue(cache);
11           }else {
12               LRU_S3_GET(index, cache);
13           }
14       }else {
15           cache = new Cache( );
16           if (exist == true){
17               LRU_S3_GET(index, cache);
18           }else {
19               create_new_index_file(index, cache);
20           }
21           hash_add(index, cache);
22       }
23       return cache;
24   }
```

Listing 6.2   LRU_get_cache(index)

❷ This *LRU_get_cache()* function is used to get the cache structure.

❹ We call the RAFT module to get the revision number and hash value of the index file, the store the revision number and hash value of files with RAFT protocol, which is the distributed consistence algorithm to do guarantee that all YunFS running nodes have the same value at the same time. This key value will automatically synchronize. If some value changed, all the instances of YunFS will get the notification that some key values have changed, due to it we need take some update with the cache. So we can call the *raft_get_rev_hash()* to get the newest key&hash value.

❺ Getting the cache structure by using the hash table. If the cache has a value, it means that we have already cached the structure, so we need to take a revision and a hash which is compared with the rev &hash obtained by RAFT. If the comparison is same, we can say that the cache is fresh, we can use this cache directly. However, if the cache is not fresh, we need call *LRU_S3_GET()* function to download the file from the remote cloud storage.

⓮ If the cache is null, we can take an allocation with the cache, then we need check the exist variable which is returned by the *raft_get_rev_hash()* function. The exist means that the RAFT has already stored the rev&hash. If we don't have this index file, we would not obtain its rev&hash, because the YunFS is in block chain structure when storing the data. If file's exists is true, we can download the file from remote cloud storage. If not true, we need to create this new index file, and this new index file will be uploaded to remote cloud storage. The last line is to add this new created cache into the hash table, in the end, we can access it later by using the hash algorithm.

6.2.2 disk write

```
1
2   function LRU_write(offset, buf, size)
3   {
4       var index = offset/FILE_SIZE;
5       var file_offset = (offset - index*FILE_SIZE)%FILE_SIZE
            ;
6       var cache = LRU_get_cache(index);
7       fseek(cache->fp, file_offset, SEEK_SET);
8       count = fwrite(buf, 1, size, cache->fp);
9       LRU_dirty_queue_add(cache);
10      return count;
11  }
```

Listing 6.3   LRU_write(offset, but, size)

❷ The function *LRU_write()* is used to write something to the storage, and it will be actually stored in the remote cloud storage.

❹ The implementation logic of this function is almost same as the function *LRU_read()*, the only difference is that in *LRU_write()* the cache will be queued to dirty queue which will be scheduled periodically to push the local modified index file to remote cloud storage. This feature will be introduced in next *disk_recycle* function.

6.2.3 disk recycle

```
1
2   function LRU_recycle()
3   {
4       while(cache = LRU_dirty_queue_get()){
5           LRU_push(cache);
6       }
7       if (LRU_get_cache_count() < RECYCLE_THREOD){
8           return;
9       }
10      for (i = 0; i < RECYCLE_COUNT; i++){
11          cache = LRU_get_last_cache();
12          LRU_clear_cache(cache);
13      }
```

```
14  }
```

Listing 6.4 LRU_recycle()

❷ The *LRU_recycle()* is called at period time, the main target of this function is to take a clean with the dirty cache and least recently used cache.

❹ Getting the cache from the dirty queue, then push those locally modified files, then store the index file to remote cloud storage.

❼ Checking whether the cache count is less than RECYCLE_THREOD or not. If we don't touch the throttle max, it needs not to call the recycle function but just to return directly.

❿ Taking a clean with the least recently used cache, at first it will obtain the least recently used cache, then clean it from local by freeing the cache memory and deleting the index file downloaded from remote cloud storage.

```
1
2   function LRU_push(cache)
3   {
4       hash = sha(cache->fp);
5       if (cache.hash == hash){
6           return;
7       }
8
9       cache.rev = cache.rev+1
10      cache.hash = hash;
11
12      upload_file(cache.fp);
13      raft_set_rev_hash(cache.index, cache.rev, cache.hash);
14  }
```

Listing 6.5 LRU_push(cache)

❷ This function *LRU_push()* is used to update the local cache file to remote cloud storage.

❹ Take a hash with local index file, then take comparable with original hash. If the comparison is equal, it means that the index file is not modified, and will be returned directly.

❼ Next is to update the rev number. The rev number is not a necessary if we already use the hash value, such as GIT's commit id. However, with rev number, we can well understand the concrete rev number of the index file. It is better than uniquely being a random hash value.

⓬ Uploading the index file to remote cloud storage, in this *upload_file()* function, it will call the REST or CLI command which is provided by the cloud storage company to upload the file to remote cloud storage.

⓭ This line of code is to call the RAFT consistency protocol function to store the rev and hash in distributed table. It is noticed that when one YunFS node calls this *raft_set_rev_hash()* function, all the other nodes of YunFS will update this distributed table. We use RAFT to resolve the consistence issue.

6.2.4 disk existence

```
1
2  function LRU_exist()
3  {
4       exist = raft_get_rev_hash(0);
5       return exist;
6  }
```

Listing 6.6   LRU_exist()

❷ *LRU_exist()* is used to check whether YunFS is created or not, it will return false only at the first time of using YunFS. This is the original of YunFS.

6.2.5 asynchronous update callback

```
1
2  function LRU_update(index, rev, hash)
3  {
4       var cache = hash_find(index);
5
6
7       if (cache != NULL){
8            if (rev != cache.rev || hash != cache.hash){
9                 LRU_GET(index, cache);
10           }
11      }
12 }
13
14
15 init()
16 {
17      raft_register_callback(LRU_update);
18 }
```

Listing 6.7   LRU_update(index, rev, hash)

❷ This is the asynchronous callback function, when the distributed table is updated, it means that one node of YunFS modifies an index file.

❼ If we do have the cache in local storage, we need have a comparison with the rev and hash. If the comparison is not equal, we need to update the local stored index file by downloading the new index file from remote cloud storage.

⓱ Register the callback function to the Raft module in the initiating function,

CHAPTER 7

THE DISTRIBUTED CONSISTENCE MODULE DESIGN

7.1 The Brief Description of the Distributed Data Consistence

In this chapter, we will begin to talk about the consensus problem, which is a classical problem in distributed systems. As a distributed system, there are many nodes running together to build up a large system, the policy to handle the distributed system is that divide a big problem into pieces then take conquer with those pieces. When I design this distributed module, the first issue is how to synchronize data consistency with all nodes. We may take some modifications with one node's data, but how to keep them synchronized with other nodes? Besides this, when one node wants to query information like getting the content of a file, all nodes should get same information no matter where they are. To resolve this consistence issue, we introduce a consensus algorithm into this YunFS system.

I want to tell the background before introducing our present used consensus algorithm. I came from China, an East County with a very long history. People who lived there are more familiar with the management of an emperor. The only leader of the country is an emperor, some ministers help the emperor to manage the people and the country. From this background, you can understand why I invent the consensus algorithm which is the emperor algorithm.

The leader is the emperor who controls something like Yuchi to indicate his power, minister and civilian are the person who have the possibility to become the emperor. If he owns the Yuchi, he is the leader of the country, no matter how he wins, by revolution, revelation or anything else.

It is the emperor who owns the most strongest power, this is the basic feature of the emperor. I also design a hash cash algorithm to indicate the power, anybody who is the first one to obtain the correct result by using hash cash algorithm. Is this algorithm look like Bitcoin's hash cash algorithm? Yes indeed, they are same algorithm, I use Bitcoin's hash cash algorithm to take a decision who can become the leader. As a leader, he has the right of writing. However, followers only have the right of reading. One writer and multiple readers. The log entry is append only, it does not provide a replacing feature. To replace the old one, it is more like to add a new entry to log.

From above steps, you notice that it is more like RAFT algorithm which is invented by two PhD. Students of Stanford university in 2014. The RAFT is one leader multiple followers policy, the append log entry. The RAFT has three roles in its algorithm, the leader,candidates and followers. If the leader is absent or does something wrong that lost the connections with other followers, every follower can become a candidate to begin its voting procedures. The candidate who wins the majority of votes in a voting procedure can become the leader, all others will become followers. The leader will keep the heart beat with his followers, if one follower lost the connection with the leader, the leader will mark the lost connection follower as offline, until this follower reconnects to the leader. The leader will pass the missing log entries to this reconnected followers. From above descriptions we can well know the logic of the RAFT algorithm which is more easy to be understood than PASOX or zoo keeper algorithm. Because the Europeans can more familiar with the democracy, the RAFT algorithm adopts the voting algorithm, anybody can become the leader if he obtains enough votes. This is the main difference between the RAFT algorithms and my own emperor algorithm. I want to mention that the Bitcoin is invented by an Eastern person who adopts the computing power. So in future, if someone invents another algorithm to replace Bitcoin algorithm, I think they will probably adopt the voting algorithm. In the end, I still adopt the RAFT algorithm in YunFS, because of its most rigorous design. Anyway the emperor algorithm needs more time to finish a perfect design, sooner or later the emperor algorithm will be published in an interesting way.

Figure 7.1 Bamboo may bend but will not break

The RAFT is motivated to take an alternative to PAXOS. The PAXOS is very difficult to be understood and hard to be implemented by following its theory. Due to it, two PhD. Students of Stanford University invent a comparable simple consensus algorithm that is RAFT. The features of the RAFT are listed below.

- Stronger leader
  The leader does most of the work, issues all log updates. Raft achieves consensus via an elected leader. A server in a raft cluster is either a leader, a candidate, or a follower. The leader is responsible for log replication to the followers. It regularly informs the followers of its existence by sending a heartbeat message. Each follower has a timeout (typically between 150 and 300 ms) in which it expects the heartbeat from the leader. The timeout is reset on receiving the heartbeat. If no heartbeat is received the follower changes its status to candidate and starts a new leader election.

- Leader election
  Use a random timer to elect leaders. A leader election starts with a candidate server. A server becomes a candidate if it receives no heartbeat from the leader within the timeout. It starts the election by increasing the term counter and

sending a Request Vote message to all other servers. The other servers will vote for the first candidate that sends them a RequestVotemessage. A server will only vote once per term. If the candidate receives a message from a leader with a term number equal or larger than the current term, then its election is defeated and the candidate changes into a follower. If a candidate receives a majority of votes, then it becomes the new leader. If neither happens, e.g., because of a split vote, then a new leader election is started after a timeout. The timeout values of each server should be spread out within a reasonable interval. This should reduce the chance of a split vote because servers won't become candidates at the same time.

- Log replication
  The leader is responsible for the log replication. It accepts client requests. The requests are forwarded to the followers in AppendEntries messages. Once the leader receives confirmation from the majority of its followers the request is considered committed.

7.2   The basic function of RAFT In YunFS

7.2.1   check_is_raft_leader

```
1
2   function check_is_raft_leader()
3   {
4       var leader;
5       leader = raft_get_current_leader();
6       if (leader == 'None'){
7           return false;
8       }else if (leader == 'Leader'){
9           return true;
10      }else {
11          return false;
12      }
13
14  }
```

Listing 7.1   check_is_raft_leader()

❷ *check_is_raft_leader()* is used to take a check whether the current node is a leader or not. It will call the RAFT library's interface function *raft_get_current_leader()*. If the current node is a leader, will return Leader. If not, will return None.

7.2.2   get_raft_leader_info

```
1
2  function get_raft_leader_info()
3  {
4      var leader;
5      var peer = {};
6      leader = raft_get_current_leader();
7
8      node = raft_get_node(leader)
9      peer_conn = raft_node_get_udata(node)
10
11     peer = {'peer_host': peer_conn.raft_addr,
12             'peer_port': peer_conn.raft_port}
13
14     return peer;
15 }
```

Listing 7.2   get_raft_leader_info()

❷ *get_raft_leader_info()* will return Leader's information, such as its peer host
IP address and port. By obtaining the Leader's IP address and port, the
follower can quickly redirect the request to the Leader. It can save the
client's time, the follower is acting as a proxy which can forward the request
of the client to the Leader. Sometime only the Leader has the privilege of
writing, so if a follower accepts the request of writing from the client, the
follower has to forward this writing request to the Leader.

7.2.3 set_raft_log

```
1
2  function set_raft_log(key, value)
3  {
4      var leader = raft_get_current_leader()
5
6      if (leader != 'Leader'){
7          return false;
8      }
9
10     var entry = {"id":rand(),
11                  "buf": key+':'value
12                 }
13
14     resp = raft_recv_entry(entry);
15     if (resp == null){
16         return false;
17     }
18     var done = 0;
```

```
19
20      do {
21          resp = raft_msg_entry_response_committed();
22          switch (resp) {
23              case 0:
24                  break;
25              case 1:
26                  done = 1;
27                  break;
28              case -1:
29                  return false;
30          }
31      } while (!done)
32
33      return true;
34  }
```

Listing 7.3   set_raft_log(key value)

❷ The function *set_raft_log(key value)* is a privilege function which can only be operated by Leader, it will check whether the current node is Leader or not. Only the Leader can continue.

❿ The Leader encapsulates the entry id with random numbers and pass this entry to all the followers. After it, the leader will wait for the entry is committed by the followers. This is a blocking function, it will loop to wait for the entry's commission to be committed. All this done, it will return.

7.2.4 get_raft_log

```
1
2  function get_raft_log(key)
3  {
4      return hash_get(key);
5  }
```

Listing 7.4   get_raft_log(key)

❷ The function *get_raft_log(key)* is easy, it will query the hash cache to get the value of the key and return this value back to the client.

❹ It is an easy way to the hash table to store the key and value into memory, sometime it will store its memory data to disk to save memory and this is Demand Request.

Figure 7.2   Are you lucky to read this book?

Index

www.ingramcontent.com/pod-product-compliance
Lightning Source LLC
Chambersburg PA
CBHW060151060326
40690CB00018B/4065